ENGLISCH IM BERUF

English for Customer Care

Rosemary Richey

SHORT COURSE
SERIES

Verfasserin	Rosemary Richey, München
kritische Durchsicht	Britta Landermann, Steinhagen John Sydes, München
Verlagsredaktion Redaktionelle Mitarbeit Bildredaktion Gesamtgestaltung und technische Umsetzung	Janan Barksdale Christine House, Christoph Moors M.A., Fritz Preuss (Wortliste), Sarah Smith Uta Hübner Sylvia Lang

Bildquellen

Titelfoto: Getty Images/PhotoAlto (RF)
Fotos: Alamy Images: S. 48/J. Powell Photographer; Banana Stock: S. 22, 24, 25, 27, 30, 55;
Comstock: S. 29, 55; Corbis GmbH: S. 32/R. Lewine, S. 37, 51, 54, 55/C. Savage; Das Fotoarchiv:
S. 16/A. Buck, 18/A. Buck; Getty Images: S. 5, 11, 15, 21, 30, 34/altrendo images, 38, 47, 48/J. Dewey,
57; Zefa: S. 5/Masterfile (2)/M. Thomsen, 12/M. Thomsen, 42/C. Goerling, 48/Grace
Symbole: Andreas Terglane, Kassel
Cartoons und Illustrationen: Oxford Designers and Illustrators

Nicht alle Copyright-Inhaber konnten ermittelt weren; deren Urheberrechte werden hiermit
vorsorglich und ausdrücklich anerkannt.

Wir danken für die freundliche Abdruckerlaubnis: S. 5 Amazon.de GmbH (Amazon, Amazon.com,
Amazon.de, das Amazon.com Logo und dasAmazon.de Logo sind registrierte Marken und „and
you're done" ist eine Marke von Amazon.com, Inc. oder deren Tochtergesellschaften.)

www.cornelsen.de

1. Auflage, 5. Druck 2011

Alle Drucke dieser Auflage sind inhaltlich unverändert und können im Unterricht nebeneinander verwendet werden.

© 2005 Cornelsen Verlag, Berlin

Druck: CS-Druck CornelsenStürtz, Berlin

ISBN 978-3-464-01882-8

 Inhalt gedruckt auf säurefreiem Papier aus nachhaltiger Forstwirtschaft.

Inhalt

Vorwort

English for Customer Care wurde speziell für Beschäftigte im Bereich Kundenservice entwickelt, die für Ihre tägliche Arbeit gute Englischkenntnisse benötigen. Ob in der Verkaufsabteilung oder im Kundenservice eines Unternehmens, ob im direkten Kundenkontakt in einem Geschäft, einer Bank oder in einem Hotel oder aber am Telefon bei einer *Hotline* oder im Call-Center: Wer erfolgreich mit Kunden kommunizieren möchte, benötigt die richtigen sprachlichen Mittel und bestimmte Techniken.

Dieser SHORT COURSE bietet nicht nur Redewendungen und Vokabeln, sondern auch Höflichkeits- und andere Strategien, die für eine effektive Verständigung in englischer Sprache in Ihrem Arbeitsbereich relevant sind.

English for Customer Care besteht aus sechs Units. Nach der ersten Unit, die eine Einführung in die Grundlagen des Kundenservice bietet, werden in den vier folgenden Units verschiedene Formen des Kundenkontakts behandelt: das persönliche Gespräch, telefonische (einschließlich typischer Situationen im Call-Center) oder schriftliche Kontakte. Die abschließende Unit stellt Ihnen die sprachlichen Mittel vor, die für effiziente Problemlösung und für das Beschwerdemanagement benötigt werden.

Jede Unit beginnt mit dem sogenannten **First approach**, der aus kurzen Übungen, *Brainstorming* oder einem Quiz besteht. Es folgen Dialoge (die sich alle auf der beiliegenden **Audio-CD** befinden), Texte und authentische Dokumente sowie eine Vielfalt von Übungen, die helfen, wichtige Vokabeln und Redewendungen im Kontext zu erlernen. In den Units wird jeweils auf die **Partner files** im Anhang verwiesen; dies sind Rollenspiele, die es Ihnen ermöglichen, den in der Unit erlernten Wortschatz in typischen Situationen mit einem Partner oder einer Partnerin zu trainieren.

In **English for Customer Care** geht es nicht nur um aktives Sprechen, sondern es werden auch Fachthemen behandelt. Jede Unit endet mit einem **Outlook**-Text, der sich inhaltlich auf das Thema der Unit bezieht und zur Diskussion anregt. **Customer focus extra**-Kästchen vermitteln Tipps und Redemittel zum korrekten und differenzierten Umgang mit Kunden.

Wenn alle Units bearbeitet sind, können Sie Ihren Kenntnisstand anhand eines Kreuzworträtsels überprüfen, mit dem das Vokabular des SHORT COURSE wiederholt wird – **Test yourself!**

Im Anhang von **English for Customer Care** finden Sie einen **Answer key**, mit dem Sie Ihre Lösungen selbstständig kontrollieren können. Der Anhang enthält außerdem die **Partner files** und eine **A–Z word list**. Mit Hilfe der Zusammenstellung von **Useful phrases and vocabulary** können Sie auch am Arbeitsplatz die häufigsten Redewendungen schnell nachschlagen.

Introduction to customer care

First approach

People have strong opinions about customer care. What is important for you as a customer? Work with a partner to make a list of the kind of services you expect.

Notes

1 Read this true customer care success story and find four word partnerships with 'customer'.

customer

Can you add any other words to make more partnerships?

amazon.de **Focus on … Amazon**

Amazon.com is one of the most successful companies on the Internet. It boasts of the latest technological website trends, but the company is especially well-known for its customer satisfaction for online shopping.

Customer convenience is the top priority at Amazon.com. Visit the site once, and when you return, Amazon.com remembers your name and when you visited the site. You can instantly see what items you have bought. It also shows where you browsed on earlier visits. The customer-friendly IT system recommends other titles or products that might be of interest the next time you shop.

At Amazon.com, top technology gives customer satisfaction. Moreover, the website helplines assist customers with any enquiry, order or even with complaints or problems. The Amazon agents are ready to give customers efficient service by email or phone.

The highest customer aim is to make shopping more convenient and enjoyable. Amazon.com wants to make sure that customers finish their transactions with a positive impression. This is essential to the continued success of Amazon.com.

VOCABULARY ASSISTANT

to assist *helfen*   to boast of sth *stolz auf etw. sein*
to browse *surfen*   convenience *Komfort*
enquiry *Anfrage*

According to the article, why is Amazon so successful?
Complete this list.

Notes

1   updated technology

2

3

4

5

2   **Find a word in the text that means the same as:**

1   to be proud of
2   the highest importance
3   to suggest
4   to help

5   fast and organized
6   easy or helpful to use
7   nice
8   very important

Now use words from above to complete these sentences.

a   Our customers' satisfaction is our top _____.

b   If you contact our call centre, one of our agents can _____ you.

c   Good communication skills are _____ in any customer care job.

d   And you can pay by credit card, which is very _____ when shopping online.

e   We can offer a quicker and more _____ level of service with our new call centre.

f   If you are happy with our products, please _____ us to a friend.

3   **You are in a meeting with a possible new customer. Answer his or her questions about your**
company with some key vocabulary from the text.

Q   What makes your company different?

A   Our company boasts of _____ [1].

We're especially well-known for _____ [2].

Q   How do you make it easy and convenient for the customer?

A   We offer convenience to the customers with

_____ [3].

Q   How do I get after-sales service?

A   We give efficient customer service by

_____ [4].

Q   What is the most important focus for your
customers?

A   Our top priority is to _____

_____ [5].

4   **Use words from the list to complete this web diagram on customer service-centred businesses and jobs.**

cashier • concierge • hotel • order entry clerk • receptionist •
representative • restaurant • sales • shop assistant • teller

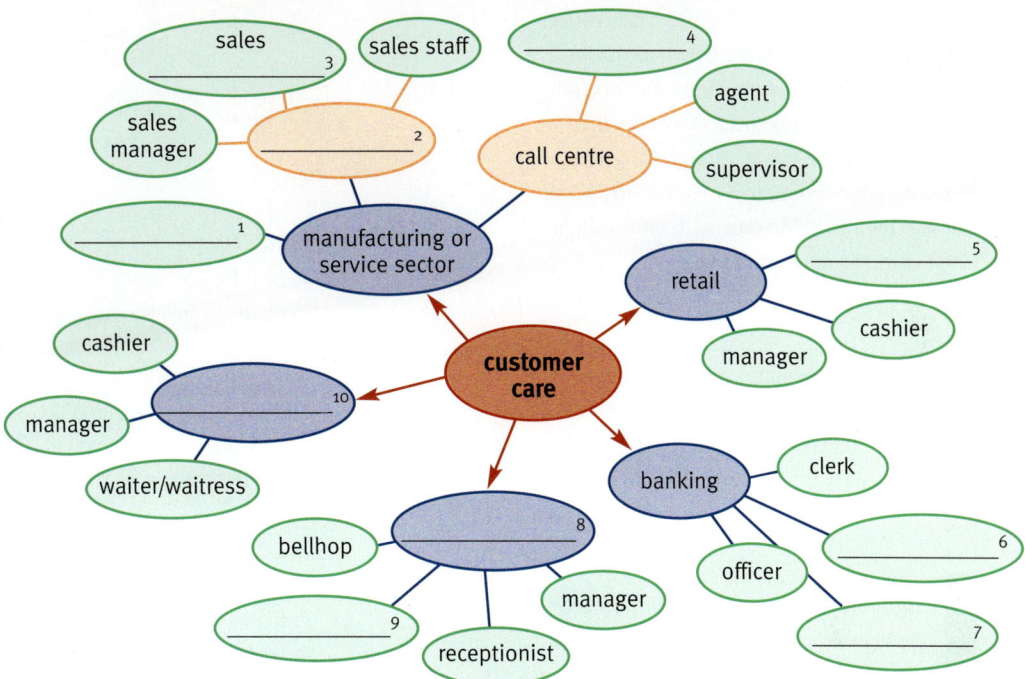

Is your job or business area on the diagram? If not, add it to the diagram. Can you add another customer care position?

5   **Now find people in the web diagram that complete the statements below. More than one answer is possible in each case. Compare your answers with a partner's.**

1   _____ deals with customers in person.

2   _____ is responsible for helping customers choose the right product.

3   _____ handles customer questions or problems over the phone.

4   _____ takes care of after-sales service.

5   _____ processes product orders for customers.

6   _____ often has to write to customers.

| VOCABULARY ASSISTANT | to deal with sb *mit jdm zu tun haben*   to handle sth *bearbeiten* to be responsible for (doing) sth *verantwortlich sein für* to take care of sb/sth *sich kümmern um* |

6 **Look at the news flash and the extracts from five job advertisements. What kind of 'people' skills do the adverts mention? Complete the notes.**

NEWS FLASH

Are technical skills enough?

Customer care is becoming more and more focused on IT training. It's true that nowadays technical skills are essential for working with customer service systems. However, this high-tech training is not enough for good customer care. Employees also need people skills so that they can deal with people in all kinds of customer situations.

Notes

1 good telephone manner

1 You must be fluent in German and English with a very good telephone manner and good customer service skills. PC skills and good communication skills are required.

2 Customer care and communication skills are essential. Ability to perform effectively under pressure and to work as part of a team.

3 Your role is to provide customers with first-class customer care. Duties: handling telephone enquiries and complaints; making calls to customers; dealing with correspondence by email and letter. Computer skills and good writing skills required.

4 We need someone with the ability to communicate clearly with customers and work effectively with both internal and external teams.

5 You will need experience in communicating face to face with customers, using tact and diplomacy.

What kind of skills do you need for your job? Write a job advert for your position.

7 **Here are some comments taken from customer service questionnaires.**
Mark them as positive P or negative N.

1 "Your sales staff is impatient. They never wait for people to finish speaking and are always in a hurry." ☐

2 "The people working at your call centre are always so polite and helpful. And they always take the time to answer all my questions." ☐

3 "I wish your employees would be more attentive. They don't seem to listen to what I say and don't care about me at all." ☐

4 "The bank officer took care of my requests straight away. I didn't have to wait at all." ☐
5 "When I arrived at your hotel, I was totally ignored by both the bellhop and the receptionist." ☐
6 "The clerk was really rude and pretended not to see me." ☐
7 "The waiter was well informed about the the menu and was prompt in bringing my food." ☐
8 "Your service was more than I asked for. That really made me feel special." ☐

8 Find words in exercise 7 to complete the table.

positive		negative	
to be attentive	1	to ignore sb	
to take the time		_____	2
polite		_____	3
_____	4	uninformed	
_____	5	too slow	
patient		_____	6
_____	7	unhelpful	
_____	8	ordinary	

> **VOCABULARY ASSISTANT**
>
> attentive *aufmerksam*
> patient *geduldig*
> to pretend *so tun, als ob*
> rude *unhöflich*

Now use words from the table to complete these sentences from a customer care handbook. Sometimes more than one answer is possible. Compare with a partner's.

a Customers always expect you to be _____ .

b If you are _____ to customers, they will not do business with you again.

c Being _____ always makes a bad impression on customers or guests.

d You should be _____ about the services or products you provide.

e A call centre agent should never be _____ on the phone and should
   always be _____ .

9 Tell your partner about one positive and one negative customer care situation you have recently experienced. Make a list of suggestions to improve negative service. Use the phrases in the box below in your discussion.

> **USEFUL LANGUAGE**
>
> | **Making suggestions** | **Responding to suggestions** |
> | --- | --- |
> | Why don't you …? | That's right./I agree. |
> | Don't/Wouldn't you agree that …? | I see your point. |
> | Isn't it a better idea to …? | I disagree because … |
> | It makes a good/bad impression if they/you … | I don't agree. I would … |

Outlook

How much do you know about customer care? Mark the following statements agree A
or disagree D **. Then read the article to see how your answers compare.**

☐ 1 Customers do not tell their friends and colleagues about bad customer care experiences.

☐ 2 The product itself is more important than the service behind it.

☐ 3 Good, friendly service will keep customers coming back.

☐ 4 After the sale is finished, the customer does not need any attention.

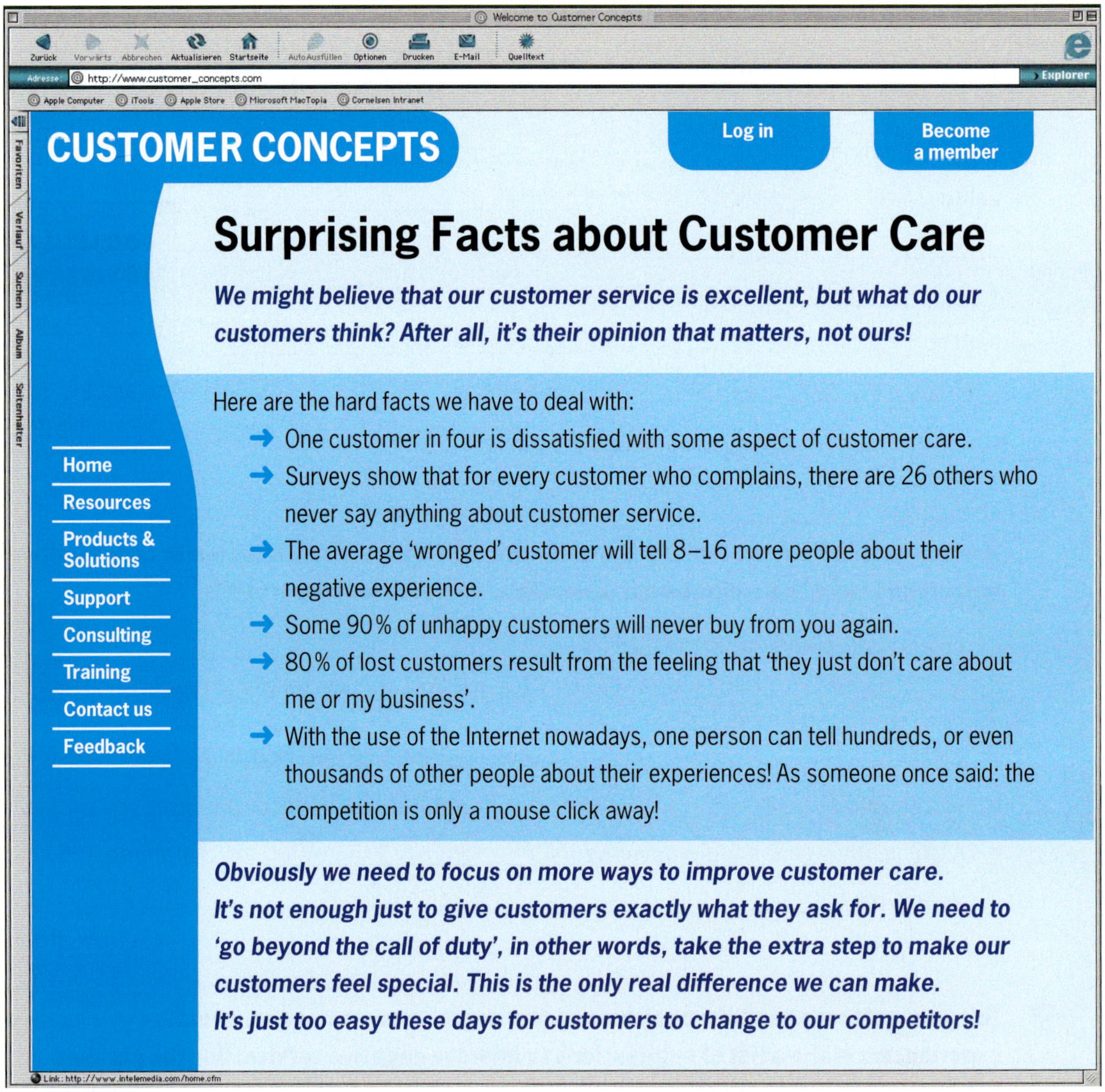

CUSTOMER CONCEPTS

Log in | Become a member

Surprising Facts about Customer Care

We might believe that our customer service is excellent, but what do our customers think? After all, it's their opinion that matters, not ours!

Home
Resources
Products & Solutions
Support
Consulting
Training
Contact us
Feedback

Here are the hard facts we have to deal with:

→ One customer in four is dissatisfied with some aspect of customer care.

→ Surveys show that for every customer who complains, there are 26 others who never say anything about customer service.

→ The average 'wronged' customer will tell 8–16 more people about their negative experience.

→ Some 90% of unhappy customers will never buy from you again.

→ 80% of lost customers result from the feeling that 'they just don't care about me or my business'.

→ With the use of the Internet nowadays, one person can tell hundreds, or even thousands of other people about their experiences! As someone once said: the competition is only a mouse click away!

Obviously we need to focus on more ways to improve customer care.
It's not enough just to give customers exactly what they ask for. We need to 'go beyond the call of duty', in other words, take the extra step to make our customers feel special. This is the only real difference we can make.
It's just too easy these days for customers to change to our competitors!

Link : http://www.intelemedia.com/home.cfm

Over to you

If customer care is so important, why do so many businesses not pay attention to it?

Will there be more of a demand for good customer service in the future? Why or why not?

How does your company know if it is giving good or bad service?

Key concept

When you lose customers, you lose profits.
When you keep customers, you create profits!

2 Face to face with customers

First approach

What makes the most impact in face-to-face encounters in customer care? Choose the three most important aspects for you and compare your answer with a partner's.

> clear speaking voice • good vocabulary • sense of humour • expensive clothes • pleasant body language • good eye contact • accurate grammar • good grooming

1 **First read this tip from an American customer care website. Do you agree? Why or why not?**

> **What customers really notice**
> Your body language – the way you stand or sit, what you do with your arms and hands, whether you are smiling or frowning, and so on – tells the real truth to your customers! Your words may be able to hide that you're bored or uninterested, but your body can't. When meeting a customer, make eye contact within 10 seconds. This creates a bond between you and the customer and it shows your interest in real communication. If you don't make eye contact, the customer could think that you aren't interested – or even worse, that you're ignoring him or her!

Now decide whether the following body language would give a positive P or negative N impression to your customers.

1 ☐

4 ☐

6 ☐

2 ☐

3 ☐

5 ☐

7 ☐

Do you think this impression is the same for people from all cultures?

2 **Listen to these greetings in typical customer care situations, and decide where they take place.**

2–6

☐ a trade fair ☐ a bank ☐ a shop ☐ a company ☐ a hotel

Now listen again and complete these sentences. Which sentences can be used when you a) meet someone new b) meet someone you already know c) offer help and d) ask someone to do something?

1 Good morning, Ms Richards. _____?

2 Well, if you need help, just _____ .

3 _____ just fill in this form, please, Mr Rodriguez?

4 Hello. _____ I help you?

5 Nice to _____ , Mr Alle.

3 **Listen to this start and finish of a company visit and complete the gaps. How well does Peter know his two hosts, Fritz and Anke? Has he met them before?**

7

Fritz Good morning, you _____[1] Peter Manser. I'm Fritz Heinle. Welcome to IGS.

Peter Thank you. It's nice to finally meet you face to face.

Fritz Yes, we've talked so much on the phone, I feel like I know you already. Peter, I'd like to

_____[2] you to Anke Schmidt, our customer services manager. Anke, this is Peter

Manser from TopForm, in Bristol.

Peter Nice to meet you, Ms Schmidt.

Anke _____[3] to meet you, too.

Fritz So, if you'd just come this way …

Anke _____[4] your flight from Bristol?

Peter It was fine. It even arrived a bit early.

Anke And is this your first time in Hamburg?

Peter No, it's my third. I've been here a couple of times as a tourist. I really like the city.

Fritz So, here we are. _____[5] your coat?

Peter Oh, that's very kind of you.

Fritz If _____[6] to take a seat …

Peter Thank you.

Fritz _____[7] care for coffee or tea?

Peter Tea would be nice, with two sugars.

■ ■ ■

Peter So, here's my taxi. Well, _____[8] for a good meeting. It was great to meet both of you.

Fritz The same for us. Thanks for _____[9]. It was a very productive meeting. So, we'll be in contact by email as usual.

Peter Yes, of course. Bye.

Anke Have a nice _____[10]! Bye.

Fritz So long for now.

Now add phrases from the dialogue to fit the categories below.

Greetings and introductions

Good morning. You must be … . I'm …

_____

_____

_____

_____

_____

Small talk questions

_____

_____

Offering hospitality

_____

_____

_____

Saying goodbye

_____

_____

_____

_____

So long for now.

4 **Complete the sentences with words from the box below.**

> care • contact • finally • get • introduce • journey • kind •
> like • long • may • pleasure

1 May I _____ you to Mrs Berg? She's our regional manager.

2 It's nice to _____ meet you face to face.

3 _____ I take your jacket?

4 Oh, that's very _____ of you.

5 I'd _____ to introduce myself. My name's Ralf Linmann. I'm the floor manager here.

6 Would you _____ for coffee or tea?

7 Can I _____ you some mineral water?

8 We'll be in _____ by email as usual.

9 It was a _____ to meet you. Have a nice _____.

10 So _____ for now.

CUSTOMER FOCUS EXTRA

Small talk may seem to deal with unimportant topics, but it's necessary for 'breaking the ice' with customers. People can relax and get comfortable with light topics such as …
- their trip (*How was your flight? Did you have any trouble finding us?*)
- where they're staying (*So, how's your hotel? Everything OK?*)
- (first) impressions of the city (*Have you ever been to … ? So, what do you think of … so far?*)
- the weather (*Great weather, isn't it? How's the weather in … ?*)

Be careful with making small talk on topics like family, religion, politics or with making compliments about somebody's appearance. Depending on your customers' cultural background, they might find the topics too aggressive or too personal in a business context.

5 **Match items from the three columns to make mini 'small talk' conversations.**

1	So, have you ever been to Vienna before?	a	Yes, no problem. It's a very nice location here, isn't it?	A	That's good. We've been having a bit of trouble with the trains. They always seem to be late.
2	How was your trip?	b	Actually, they're both on holiday now. In Portugal.	B	You're lucky. It's been raining here for three days now. Very depressing.
3	Did you find us OK?	c	Yes, I have. I was here four years ago.	C	Me too. In fact, I'm playing in a tournament this weekend.
4	How was the weather in London?	d	Yes, I play in a local team.	D	How lovely. I was in Portugal two years ago. Do you know it?
5	So, how are Pat and John doing? Are they still working hard?	e	It was fine. The train was a bit late but we arrived on time.	E	Oh, really? Was that for business or pleasure?
6	Oh, are you interested in tennis?	f	Nice, actually. It was sunny and warm when I left.	F	Yes, we like it. We've been here for four years now.

6 **Work with a partner to practise meeting a customer for the first time. Use the flow chart below or make a dialogue that fits your own situation.**

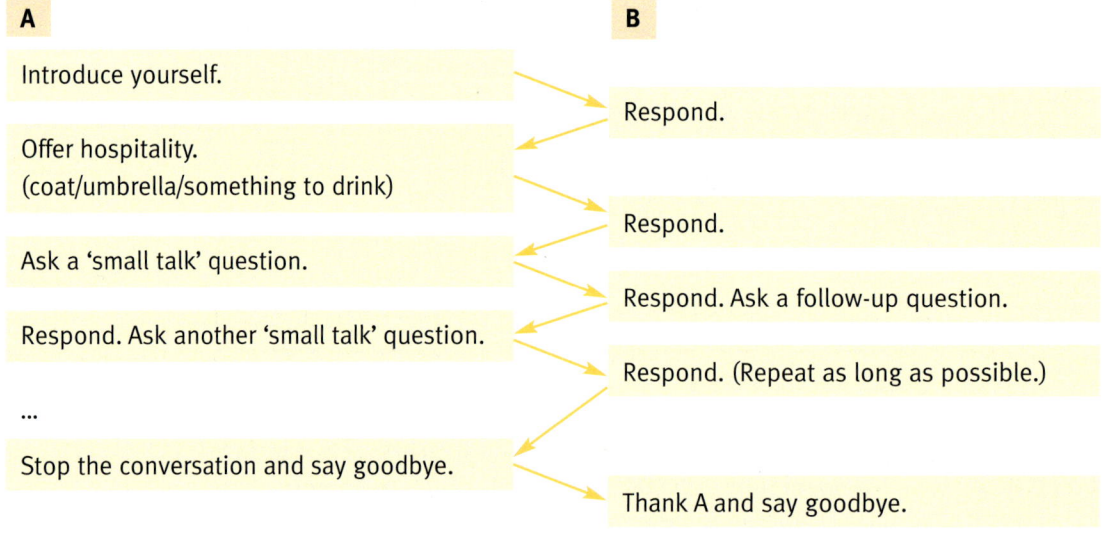

A

Introduce yourself.

Offer hospitality.
(coat/umbrella/something to drink)

Ask a 'small talk' question.

Respond. Ask another 'small talk' question.

...

Stop the conversation and say goodbye.

B

Respond.

Respond.

Respond. Ask a follow-up question.

Respond. (Repeat as long as possible.)

Thank A and say goodbye.

CUSTOMER FOCUS EXTRA

Good basic socializing skills help build your customer base. From the beginning, your customers will see how you show interest and pay attention. This is an important step in establishing a rapport with your customers.

7   **Look at this text from a customer care manual and fill in the missing *do's* and *don'ts*.**

Meetings are an important tool for building your customer base. They provide a great opportunity to network with your customers for future business. Look at these do's and don'ts for successful customer meetings.

- *Do*_____ prepare for your meeting.

- *Do*_____ make sure you know about all your products or services.

- *Don't*_____ take control of the discussion. _____ let the customers decide what they talk about and when they talk about it.

- _____ give customers only the information they want. _____ overwhelm them with extra information that they don't really need.

- _____ use jargon or words only people in your company or industry know.

- _____ talk more than your customers. _____ listen carefully to what they say and _____ interrupt them.

- _____ ask for feedback and clarification, so you'll know exactly what your customers want and need.

- _____ be open, honest, flexible and positive!

VOCABULARY ASSISTANT	clarification *Erläuterungen* to interrupt *unterbrechen* jargon *Fachsprache* to overwhelm *überfordern*

Can you add any other helpful tips based on your meetings with customers?

8   **Look at these pairs of sentences and say which one would be more effective in a meeting. Refer to the do's and don'ts in exercise 7.**

1   a   OK, let's get started. Unfortunately, I've got another appointment in an hour.
    b   Thanks for coming today. I'm glad to help you review your business needs.
2   a   As I understand it, you'd like to discuss …
    b   This is what we're going to talk about …
3   a   So, that was my suggestion. Is that suitable for you? I'd like to get your feedback.
    b   So, that's the right service for you. I don't think we need to discuss this anymore.
4   a   OK, we'd better stop now. I really must go to my next meeting.
    b   Let's go over our action points once more. I want to be sure we agree.
5   a   I've done some research into your company. It seems you …. Is that right?
    b   So, can you tell me something about your company?
6   a   I don't think we can do that. We never offer that kind of discount.
    b   I'll see what I can do.

9 Work with a partner. Use the information in your file (or make up your own) to role-play a meeting from first greetings to goodbyes.

PARTNER FILES   Partner A   File 01, p. 58
Partner B   File 01, p. 60

 10 Listen to this conversation at a trade fair between a sales rep and a potential customer and say whether the following statements are true ☐T☐ or false ☐F☐, or you don't know ☐?☐.

1 Lewis has made an appointment to meet Otto at the stand. ☐

2 This is Otto's fifth time at the trade fair. ☐

3 Lewis is interested in a particular product. ☐

4 Otto gives Lewis a catalogue to take back to his company. ☐

5 Lewis agrees to put his name on the mailing list. ☐

6 Otto will telephone Lewis in two weeks to set up a follow-up appointment. ☐

Write Otto's notes about the meeting with Lewis. What does he need to do when he is back in the office?

 Accutech UK
25 Bridge St
Wisbech, Cambridgeshire
PE13 5JP

Lewis Gillan
Account Manager

Tel +44 1945 579235
Fax +44 1945 579266
email gillan@accutech.uk.com

Notes
_____
_____
_____
_____
_____

 11 Complete these extracts from the dialogue. Then listen again to check your answers.

anything • ask • brochure • email • enjoying • free • glad •
introduce • mind • put

1 May I _____ myself? I'm Otto Brandt. I work for Metro GmbH. May I _____ your name?

2 So, Mr Gillan, how are you _____ the trade fair?

3 Well, then, are you looking for _____ in particular?

4 OK, but please feel _____ to ask me any questions. I'd be _____ to go over our products and try to find something suitable for your company.

5   Ah, can I interest you in a _____? It has information about our company and our full range of products.

6   Would you like to _____ your name on our mailing list?

7   Do you _____ if I take your business card? I'll make sure you're on our list. And here's my card. I'll send you a quick _____ next week to see if I can help you with any of our products.

12   **Rewrite the following sentences to make them more polite and effective. Look back at the dialogue for ideas.**

1   Who are you?
2   What are you looking for?
3   Ask me a question if you want.
4   Do you want a brochure?

5   I'll put your name on the mailing list, OK?
6   Give me your business card.
7   I'll contact you sometime soon.

CUSTOMER FOCUS EXTRA

Follow-up is your most important tool for success for any face-to-face encounter. Be sure to be specific about what you will do for your customer and when you will do it.

Use 'I'll + infinitive' to tell the customer of your next action:
I'll write you a quick email next week.
I'll send you the latest brochure tomorrow.
NOT: I write you .../I send you ...

Use 'would you mind if + the simple past', 'do you mind + the simple present' or 'may + infinitive (without to)' to ask if something is acceptable or not.
Would you mind if I phoned you on Monday?
Do you mind if I ask you some questions about your company?
May I stop by your office next week?

Remember, good customer care means taking action to support your words! This builds trust into your customer relationships.

---

13   **Match the questions to the right response.**

1   Would you mind if I put your name on our mailing list?
2   I'll just note that in my diary.
3   Do you mind if I give you my card?
4   I'm afraid I don't have the information here. But I'll call my office and get back to you this afternoon. Is that ok?
5   I'll be in Brixton on Tuesday. Would you mind if I stopped by your office?
6   May I get in touch with you next week?
7   I'll fax you the new price list tomorrow.

a   Tuesday? Yes, that sounds fine. I'll email you directions when I'm back in the office.
b   No, not at all. You can find all my contact information on my card.
c   Sure. I'll wait for your phone call on Monday.
d   Yes, that sounds good. I'll stop by the stand at around 3.
e   Thanks. That's very kind of you.
f   I'll write it down too. So, we said Monday at 10.30, right?
g   No, let me give you mine, too.

14 Work with a partner to do a role-play. First look at the useful phrases below. Then use the information in your file (or make up your own) to role-play a conversation at a trade fair.

PARTNER FILES → Partner A   File 02, p. 58
Partner B   File 02, p. 60

USEFUL PHRASES

Rep
Could/May I help you?
How can I help you?
May I introduce myself?
Could I ask your name?
Please feel free to ask me any questions.
Could I offer you/interest you in …?
Would you mind if I phoned/emailed you?
It was nice to meet you.
I hope you enjoy the fair.

Customer
No, thanks. I'm just looking/browsing.
I'm looking for/interested in …
My name's …
Nice/Pleased to meet you.
Thank you.
No, not at all. Let me give you my card/address/number.
Nice to meet you, too. I look forward to hearing from you.
Thanks, it was a pleasure. I appreciate your help.

---

15 Paula Johnston is giving a presentation at a trade fair. Put a–e in the correct order. Then listen to check your answers.

9

- [ ] a "Before I finish, I'll just go over the highlights of this presentation again. Our product and service line includes … . We stand out from our competitors with our excellent follow-up."

- [ ] b "With our impressive line of products and services, we offer special benefits that you can't find with our competitors. Follow-up is our top priority … "

- [ ] c "Thanks for your attention. I look forward to having you as a new customer."

- [ ] d "Hello, I'm Paula Johnston from Delta Systems. I'm here today to let you know about some great offers in customer care support services. I'll be speaking about our extensive range of products for tracking new and existing customers …"

- [ ] e "I hope you'll pick up one of our leaflets. Also, if you leave me your contact details, I'll be glad to send you our latest catalogue by the end of the week. And if you would like to order today, I'll make sure you receive our introductory price."

CUSTOMER FOCUS EXTRA
- Be natural in your trade fair talk. Don't use memorized speech.
- Follow up quickly. Don't delay in replying to your customers.
- Your customers will remember *you* more than your product or service!

16   **Look at the following steps for giving an effective presentation. Match the steps to the phrases.**

Steps for Winning Customers
in Your Presentations

1   Welcome the audience
2   Introduce the subject and give a brief overview
3   Talk about the main product/service features
4   Explain the unique selling points (USPs)
5   Invite interest in the company (products/services)
6   Give promotional information
7   Offer incentives to try a product
8   Finish the talk
9   Show follow-up

a   Step 2
I'd like to give you a short preview of my presentation …
We'd like to introduce/show you our latest …

b
I'll be glad/pleased to send you … by next Monday.
I'll be in contact/touch with you in two weeks.
I look forward to doing business with you.

c
We stand out from our competitors because …
Our USPs are …

d
I'd like to welcome you to …
Thank you for coming today.
My name's …
I work for … and I'm in charge of …

e
Please feel free to pick up a brochure/leaflet/free sample.
We've got our promotional information and samples available here.

f
I'd like to offer a special introductory price/discount if you order today.

g
Our product range includes …
The special highlights are …

h
We'd be pleased/glad to have you as a new customer.
We'd welcome the chance to do business with your company.

i
I'd just like to sum up the main points of today's presentation …
Thank you for your kind attention.

Now follow the steps to prepare a short presentation on one of your company's products or services. Try to use the phrases above in your talk.

Outlook

Read this article from a customer care research site and discuss the questions.

When the customer feels 'invisible'...

A recent study showed the number of seconds people had to wait to be greeted in typical customer care situations. Customers in various shops or businesses were asked how long they had been waiting. In each case, the customer thought that he/she had been waiting longer than the actual time that had passed. 30 or 40 seconds felt like three or four minutes!

Time goes by slowly when you are waiting to be noticed. With the Internet nowadays, people expect quick, almost instant responses. In face-to-face encounters, if you can't give customers immediate attention, they'll leave straight away. Businesses simply cannot afford to treat their customers as if they are 'invisible'.

The solution to this problem is clear. A prompt greeting, especially with a smile, makes all the difference to your customers. They can start the conversation or meeting with the feeling that they are an important customer for your business. Without the greeting, the customers will already be feeling uncomfortable and insecure – even before the encounter actually begins.

A quick, friendly greeting relaxes the customer and sets the right atmosphere for good customer care!

Over to you

Have you ever been ignored – or treated as if you were 'invisible' – in a customer care situation? How did you feel?

What is the impact on the customer if this happens at a presentation, trade fair or conference?

If you are busy with another customer, how can you still notice a customer and make him or her feel secure and comfortable?

Key concept Each time you make contact with customers, they are forming an opinion about your company. This is the oppportunity to create a positive image for both you and your customer-service business!

3 Dealing with customers on the phone

First approach

How well do you deal with customers on the phone? Answer the questions below for yourself, then compare your answers with a partner's.

How often do you ...	always	often	sometimes	never
1 forget the caller's name during a phone call?	☐	☐	☐	☐
2 exchange a bit of small talk with the customer?	☐	☐	☐	☐
3 have to ask the customer to repeat information?	☐	☐	☐	☐
4 forget who you put on hold?	☐	☐	☐	☐
5 take notes during the phone call?	☐	☐	☐	☐
6 have trouble remembering details of the call after you hang up?	☐	☐	☐	☐

10–11

1 **Listen to these two phone calls and say what kind of impression they make. Work with a partner to complete the table.**

What went wrong (call 1)	What went right (call 2)
_____	_____
_____	_____
_____	_____
_____	_____

Listen to the second call again. How did Martha ...

1   answer the phone? *Hello, Martha Greer speaking.* _____.

2   say she didn't understand something? *Sorry, could* _____?

3   say that there was a mistake? _____ *you've got the wrong extension, Mr Kraft.*

4   offer help? _____
    to connect you?

5   end the phone call? *I'm putting you through now.* _____.

CUSTOMER FOCUS EXTRA

Good customer-oriented telephone technique starts with being courteous. This simply means dealing with people in a respectful manner.

CUSTOMER FOCUS EXTRA

Here are some helpful tips for being courteous on the phone.

- Use polite language to show that you really care about the customer and his/her needs. With *Would you like …?* you ask the same question as with *Do you want …?* but in a more customer-friendly way.
- Use the customer's name throughout the conversation. This makes the customer feel special and helps build rapport.
- Show you are serious about taking care of the customer's requests with your good listening skills and dependable follow-through.
- Finally, don't forget to thank the customer. A simple phrase like *We appreciate your business* or *Thank you for calling* leaves a positive impression at the end of a phone call.

---

2 **Listen to the following two telephone calls between a receptionist, Elke Jähnig, and a caller from England, and complete the gaps.**

12–13

Call 1

Elke Good morning. Apex Industries. _____

_____ 1

John Yes, this is John Richards from Customer Zone Software. I'd like to speak to Eva Lang, please. Could you put me through to her?

Elke Of course, _____ 2, please. … Oh, it seems that her line is engaged. Could you hold a moment? Or _____ 3 to leave a message?

John I'd prefer to hold for just a minute or two. …

Elke Mr Richards? _____ 4. I'm putting you through to Ms Lang's office now. If you get cut off for some reason, please get back to me.

John I'm sorry. Could you speak up a bit? I didn't _____ 5 that.

Elke Sure. I'm connecting you now to Ms Lang's office. If you don't get through, please ring again. We're having some problems with our phone system.

Call 2

Elke Good morning. Apex Industries.

John This is John Richards again. _____ 6 I got cut off when you tried to put me through.

Elke I'm _____ 7 about that.

John I really need to get through to Ms Lang this afternoon. Could I leave a message for her to ring me back as soon as possible?

Elke _____ 8, Mr Richards. Could I have your phone number, please?

John	Yes, I'm calling from my mobile. It's 0044 7721 332558.

Elke   Right. So, that's 0044 7721 332558. _____ [9] she calls you back today. Could I help you with anything else?

John   Would it be possible to have her mobile number? Could you perhaps look it up for me?

Elke   Yes, that's _____ [10]. I've got it right here. It's 49 for Germany, then 156 8877944.

John   Let me just repeat that. That's 49 156 8877944.

Elke   That's right.

John   OK. Thanks once again. Bye for now.

Elke   You're welcome. Goodbye.

Now write the message that Elke takes.

☎ **Message**

Message for _____

Caller: _____

Company: _____

Message: _____
_____
_____
_____

3 **Match the statements or questions (1–8) to the responses (a–h).**

1 Thank you.
2 I'm afraid he's not in.
3 May I help you?
4 I'll make sure he gets the message straight away.
5 I'm afraid I got cut off.
6 Could I leave him a message?
7 My name is Anton Czrisinski.
8 I'm sorry. Could you spell that, please?

a Thank you. I really appreciate it.
b Yes, certainly. I'll just get a pen.
c You're welcome.
d Yes, I have a question about your price list.
e That's OK. I'll call back later.
f Yes, it's P–F–A– double-F.
g Oh, I'm terribly sorry about that. Let me put you through again.
h I'm sorry. I didn't quite catch that.

CUSTOMER FOCUS EXTRA

If you don't understand the customer, ask him or her politely to say something again or more slowly. You want to be sure you understand so that you can deal with the customer efficiently. Try phrases like:

I'm sorry, but I didn't (quite) catch that/understand you exactly.
Could we go over that once more?
Could you repeat that, please?
Could you speak a bit more slowly, please?
Could you speak up a bit, please?

4 **Complete the sentences with the correct form of the phrasal verbs from the box.**

> cut off • get back to • get through to • look up • put through • speak up

1 When I called the hotel, the operator _____ me _____ to the General Manager's office.

2 I'll _____ the address in our directory for you.

3 This is a terrible line. Could you _____ a bit, please?

4 There seems to be something wrong with his extension number. I've tried it three times and got _____.

5 It took a long time, but the customer finally _____ the help desk.

6 I'm sorry, but Ms Allen's in a meeting right now. I'll ask her to _____ you as soon as she's free.

14

5 **Choose the right words to complete the telephone conversation. Then listen to check your answers.**

Uta Edelweiss Beverages, Uta Maly.

Henry Hello. Could I have extension 226, please?

Uta I'm sorry, the line's engaged. Could you please hold/wait ¹? ... Sir, the line's free now. I'll put/pass² you through.

Henry Thanks.

Emil Service department.

Henry I'd like to tell/speak³ to Mr Schmidt, please. Is he available at the moment?

Emil Will/May⁴ I ask who's calling?

Henry Henry Jones. I'm calling from ABC Ltd in London.

Emil Just a moment please, Mr Jones. I'll see if he's available. ... Mr Jones? I'm afraid Herr Schmidt's in a meeting. Would you like to leave/list⁵ a message?

Henry Yes, please ask him to get behind/back to⁶ me as soon as possible. My number's 44 207 563 361.

Emil I'm sorry/afraid⁷ I didn't catch that. Could you repeat/say⁸ the number, please?

Henry Yes, it's 44 for the UK, then 207 563 361.

Emil OK, I'm sure/I'll make sure⁹ he gets the message. Is there anything/anyone¹⁰ else I can do for you?

Henry No, thanks.

Emil Goodbye, then, Mr Jones. Thanks for calling.

Henry Thank you. Goodbye.

6 **Work with a partner to practise a telephone call. Use the flow chart below or make a dialogue that fits your own situation.**

A	**B**
Answer the phone.	
	Say who you are and ask to speak to X. (It's urgent.)
X is in a meeting. Message?	
	Ask when the meeting finishes.
Respond. Message?	
	Leave message.
Confirm caller's name. Phone number?	
	Give your details.
Check message with caller.	
	Confirm or correct message.
Thank the caller and say goodbye.	
	Say goodbye.

7 **Listen to the telephone conversation and complete the rep's notes.**

15

☎ Called: Charles _____ 1

Time: 15 January, 2.30 pm

Company is updating the way they keep customer information and they're interested in customer tracking _____ 2.

Meeting on Wednesday, 20 January at _____ 3 pm.

_____ 4 Azan Road, Petersfield

Mobile phone: 07887 _____ 5

Email _____ 6 and brochure (PDF version)

15

Listen to the dialogue again and tick the sentences you hear.

1 a Hello, Mr Thomas, I got your contact details from one of my colleagues. ☐
  b Hello, Mr Thomas, I'm responding to your email enquiry. ☐
2 a Would Wednesday suit you? ☐
  b Could we set up a meeting for Wednesday … ? ☐
3 a Could I just confirm that I have the right address? ☐
  b Let me just make sure I have the right address. ☐
4 a Is there anything else I can do for you … ? ☐
  b How else can I help you today? ☐
5 a I look forward to seeing you on Wednesday … . ☐
  b See you on Wednesday at … . ☐

8 **Look at these basic steps for making a successful customer care phone call. Did Peter Busch follow all the steps in his phone call? If necessary, listen again to check.**

Starting the phone call

1 Identify yourself and your company
2 Say why you are calling

During the phone call

3 Use the customer's name throughout the conversation
4 Take notes of the important information
5 Ask questions to clarify information
6 Repeat and summarize

Finishing the call

7 Tell the customer what you're going to do
8 Make the customer feel confident you'll follow through
9 Offer further assistance
10 Thank the customer

Now say which steps the following sentences go with. Write the appropriate numbers in the boxes. Can you add some other sentences for each step?

Phrases

☐ a I'm calling to …
☐ b Could I just go over the details again?
☐ c Can I help you with anything else?
☐ d No problem, madam. I'll personally make sure that she calls you back today.
☐ e I'll just write that down.
1 f This is Joan Everts from Everts, Samuels and Barker.
☐ g I'll be glad to send this out to you today. You should receive it by …
☐ h Was that 50,000 or 15,000?
☐ i Hello, my name is … . I'm with Himmelhoch GmbH in Ingolstadt.
☐ j I'll check on that information with my colleague and call you back in two hours.
☐ k I appreciate you taking the time to talk to me.
☐ l OK, Mrs Armstrong. I'll just …
☐ m Let me just make a note of that.

9 **Match the sentences in A with the more customer-friendly equivalents in B.**

A

1 I'll give you a ring sometime tomorrow.
2 Nice talking to you.
3 Wait, I need to write that down.
4 What's your name?
5 I have no idea, so I really don't know what to tell you.
6 What else do you need? Is that it?
7 I'm putting it in the post today, so you'll probably get it next week.
8 I wrote it down, thanks.

B

a I'll be glad to send this out to you today. You should receive it by Tuesday.
b One moment, please. I'll just make a note of that.
c Could I take care of anything else for you today?
d May I have your name, please?
e I'll check on that information and call you back in 30 minutes.
f I appreciate you taking the time to call today.
g I'll get back to you at about 11.00 tomorrow morning. Is that OK?
h Let's go over it again to be sure of the details.

10 **Put this phone conversation in the correct order. Then listen to check your answers.**

16

Susanne Finster

☐ a Nathalie, this is Susanne Finster from Brand AG. We met at the trade fair last week.
☐ b Would Tuesday be convenient for you, at 9 am?
☐ c Bye.
☐ d Hello. May I speak to Nathalie Laurent, please?
☐ e Sounds good. OK, Nathalie, that's Tuesday at 11 o'clock. I look forward to seeing you.
☐ f Fine, thanks. Nathalie, I'm calling to see if we could set up a meeting. You wanted me to do a presentation on our services and I'll be in Metz next week.

Nathalie Laurent

☐ g Same here. Thanks for calling. Bye.
1 h Allô.
☐ i Next week? Let me just check my diary. What day exactly?
☐ j Tuesday looks good, but I'm busy at 9. How about 11 o'clock instead?
☐ k Speaking.
☐ l Ah, yes. Right. How are you?

11 **Match the questions with the appropriate response.**

1 Can we fix a meeting for next Tuesday at 9 o'clock?

2 Is Friday the 18th convenient for you?

3 Could we set up a meeting for Thursday afternoon?

4 Are you free next Monday for a meeting?

5 How about 1 o'clock at my office?

a Monday? Yes, that's fine with me.

b 1 o'clock is fine with me, but I'd prefer to meet in my office, if that's OK.

c Sorry, I've already got a meeting that morning. How about 1.30 instead?

d I'm off for a long weekend on that date. Can I ring you when I get back?

e Yes, that sounds good. Is 2 o'clock OK?

12 **Work with a partner to make two phone calls. Study the useful phrases below before you look at you role card.**

PARTNER FILES
Partner A File 03, p. 58
Partner B File 03, p. 60

USEFUL PHRASES

Arranging an appointment
Could we set up a meeting?
Are you available / free on Monday?
Does next Thursday suit you?
How about 2 pm on Tuesday?

Agreeing on a time
Just let me check my diary / planner.
Yes, Tuesday is fine with me.
Sounds good. Tuesday at 2 pm then.

Suggesting a new time
I'm sorry, but I've got another engagement.
How about Tuesday morning instead?
Actually, Thursday morning would work out better for me.

Confirming
We'll see each other next Thursday at 11.00 at your office.
Could you confirm the details in an email?
Here is my mobile number in case you need to reach me.
I look forward to seeing you.

---

13 **Use the clues to complete the puzzle and find the hidden word (something one should always try to be when dealing with customers).**

1 I'm calling to … our appointment. *(bestätigen)*

2 Thanks for … . I can put you through now.

3 Could we … … a meeting for 3 pm? *(2 words)*

4 Thanks for calling. We … your business.

5 I'm sorry. I didn't quite … what you said. Could you repeat it, please?

6 Would Monday morning be … for you? Perhaps at 9.30?

7 Could we go over that … more?

8 … care to leave a message? (2 words)

9 Can you give me her … number, please?

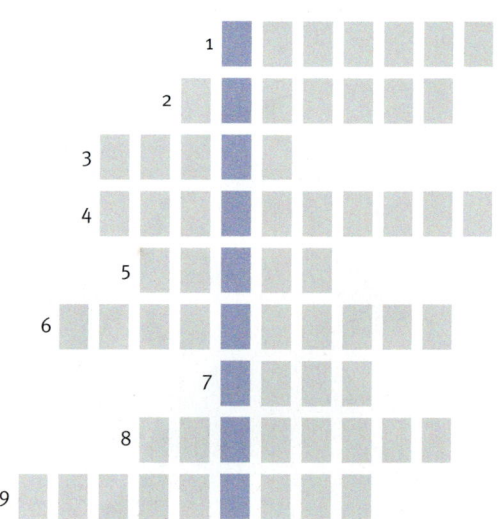

Outlook

Read this article from a customer care online magazine and answer the questions.

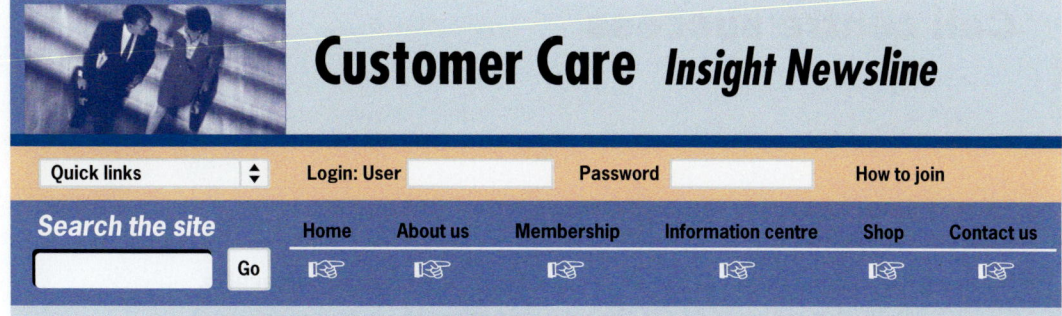

What the customers really hear ...

Customer care experts remind us to be careful of 'background noise' while dealing with customers on the phone. The phone receiver picks up even the slightest movement or noise. Keep these 'noise' awareness tips in mind:

- Don't try to talk to someone in your office while you're on the phone. The customer needs your full attention.
- Be sure to put the customer on hold if you're going to discuss something with a colleague. (Remember, always ask first before putting someone on hold.)
- Don't drink or eat during a call. The customer can hear you sipping and chewing.
- Don't smoke while talking to the customer. The customer can also hear you inhale and exhale.
- When you complete the call, hang up the phone gently. If you slam down the receiver, the customer might hear it and think you are annoyed or angry.

All these situations can give the customer the wrong message: I don't care about the customer. This can be quite embarrassing. It may even lead to the customer walking away from your business – never to return!

Over to you

Describe your own work atmosphere. What kind of 'noise' could cause a problem during your customer calls? How can you remove these distractions? Share a personal story of when you heard 'background noise' on the phone to a customer services department. What kind of impression did the business make on you?

Key concept

Good telephone technique gives the 'competitive edge' in customer care.

4 Call centre success

First approach

A survey was carried out recently on call centres for various industries in the UK. Work with a partner to select the correct answers in these survey results. Then check the key on page 64 for the answers. Were there any surprises?

1 **12% 24% 42%** of calls were rated unsatisfactory.

2 Agents were rude in **11% 21% 31%** of calls.

3 **9% 16% 25%** of calls were answered after more than 30 rings.

4 In **7% 10% 14%** of calls, agents didn't have enough knowledge to handle the call.

5 In **32% 46% 62%** of calls, agents didn't spend enough time understanding the caller's actual needs.

Would a survey in your country have similar results? Why or why not? How could call centres change the way customers rate them?

17–18

1 **Listen to the two call centre conversations. Which customer is placing an order and which has asked for help?**

Listen again and complete the table.

	Call 1	Call 2
Customer		
Customer interested in		
Follow-up		

2 **Complete these sentences from the dialogues. Listen again if necessary.**

17–18

Call 1

1   _____ that you need some assistance.

2   _____ type this in … one moment … OK.

3   As _____ it, the problem begins with entering the password. _____ ?

4   I _____ the service technicians' schedule and I _____ back in half an hour.

5   Does that sound _____ ?

6   _____ you with anything else today?

Call 2

7   One moment, _____ your customer file on my screen.

8   So, Mr Wagner, what can I _____ you?

9   I _____ your order as urgent so that the items will be sent out _____ .

10   _____ for your order. Goodbye.

CUSTOMER FOCUS EXTRA

In any call centre situation, the first impression is crucial. Customers will remember how you treated them during the first contact and it may be the only chance to show that you are willing to satisfy the customer. When customers notice professionalism and customer-focus from the very beginning, their perception of the company is a positive one. If not, their impression is negative – and usually stays that way!

Follow these tips for making a good impression:
1   Use your voice and polite language to signal a friendly 'ready-to-help' attitude.
    Gerry speaking. How can I help you today?
    What can I do for you?
    Is there anything else I can help you with today?
2   Listen carefully and make sure you understand your customers.
    I see. So, as I understand it, … . Is that correct?
    Let me just repeat that.

3   Make sure your customer understands you and is happy with the service.
    Does that sound all right?
    Do you have any other questions?
    I hope this is to your satisfaction.
4   Make promises and keep them.
    Your order will go out overnight today.
    I'll call you back in half an hour.
5   Always follow up and follow through.
    I'll ring you when the technician has finished the repair work to make sure everything is all right.

---

3 **Match the sentence halves to make complete sentences.**

1   How can I
2   I will personally make sure
3   I hope this is
4   Could you give me
5   Does that sound
6   Is there anything else
7   I'll take care
8   Let me just

a   all right?
b   of this straight away.
c   help you?
d   to your satisfaction.
e   repeat that.
f   that you receive the information this afternoon.
g   I can assist you with today?
h   your account number, please?

4   **Fill in this call centre dialogue with a suitable phrase from the list. Then listen to check your answers.**

19

could I go over your order again?

I'd just like to confirm your contact details.

Could I help you with anything else?

May I help you?

Is that right?

Could you give me your customer number, please?

OK, let me just repeat that.

Agent	Good morning. Ace Beverages Helpline. _____ 1
Customer	Yes, please. I need to place an order for ten more cases of my standard house wine – six red and four white – for my restaurant.
Agent	It sounds like you have ordered from us before. _____ _____ 2
Customer	Of course, here it is … uh … 55008-22.
Agent	Ah yes, Mr Green from Suavo Restaurant. _____ _____ 3 So, that's Breitestraße …
Customer	No, that's our old address. We've just moved to Hauptstraße 43. The postcode is still 45221 though.
Agent	_____ 4 That's Hauptstraße 43, postcode 45221. _____ _____ 5
Customer	Yes, that's right.
Agent	OK, I've updated our database. Let me just type in the order … OK …
Customer	Look, I'm really in a bind. Could you do a rush order on the wine so that we get it by this evening?
Agent	Sure, that's no problem. We can dispatch it by 11 o'clock. OK, Mr Green, _____

_____ 6. You'd like your standard order of house wine, six cases red, four white. And we'll rush the order so it arrives by approximately 5 pm.

Customer	Yes, that's correct. Thanks for helping me so quickly.
Agent	My pleasure. _____ 7
Customer	No, thank you. That's all for today. Bye for now.
Agent	Goodbye.

VOCABULARY ASSISTANT

to be in a bind *in der Klemme sein*
database *Datenbank*
rush order *Eilauftrag*

5   **Complete the sentences with words from the list.**

> catalogue • dispatched • give • invoice • overnight •
> payment • place • quote • rush

1   Are you ready to _____ your order today?
2   Are you planning to pay by transfer or credit card, or would you like to have a monthly _____ plan?
3   OK, sir, the goods are in stock and can be _____ straight away.
4   If it's urgent, we can send it as a _____ order to make sure you receive it by Thursday. Would you prefer that?
5   Can you _____ me the item number from the _____, please?
6   Let me check and call you back in one hour with a _____ on the price.
7   We'll enclose the _____ with the goods.
8   We can send the goods by _____ delivery so that you'll get them the next day.

6   **Look at the following dialogue. How would you improve the agent's language to make a good impression on the customer?**

Customer	Hello. John Norman speaking.
Agent	Please speak up. I can't understand your name. [1]
Customer	I said, this is John Norman. That's N-O-R-M-A-N.
Agent	Thanks, Mr Norman. Need some help today? [2]
Customer	I'd like to have the latest accountancy software.
Agent	The latest what? [3]
Customer	The latest accountancy software package you've got in your catalogue.
Agent	OK, how many packages do you want? [4]
Customer	I'd like five, please.
Agent	Good. Now I need your address. [5]
Customer	234 Delman Road, BN1 4QJ Brighton, England.
Agent	Fine. I've got that. Anything else? [6]
Customer	Well, when will I receive the software?
Agent	Maybe sometime next week. I've got another call coming in, so bye for now! [7]

Write customer-focused sentences to replace 1–7 above.

1   _____
2   _____
3   _____
4   _____
5   _____
6   _____
7   _____

7

20

Listen to this telephone conversation and choose the correct answers to complete the sentences.

1 The customer is calling the hotline about a problem with his MP3 player, ...
  a an i-go maxi
  b an i-go mini

2 He has ... tried to install the software.
  a already
  b not yet

3 The customer first needs to find out ... .
  a what his password is
  b what operating system his computer has

4 The customer needs ... .
  a to buy another version of the i-go
  b to upgrade his system before he installs the software

5 If the customer registers with the company, he gets ... of free service.
  a two years
  b three years

VOCABULARY ASSISTANT

free of charge *kostenlos*
system requirement *System-anforderung*

Listen again and tick the sentences you hear.

1 So, what exactly is the problem? ☐

2 Could you explain the problem in more detail? ☐

3 Could you explain what you've done so far? ☐

4 That means you need to have ... ☐

5 In other words, you need to have ... ☐

6 Do you have any questions so far? ☐

7 Are you following me all right? ☐

8 Is everything clear up to now? ☐

9 Are you having any trouble seeing that? ☐

10 Let me just talk you through the steps. ☐

11 This is what I'm going to do. ☐

12 By the way, have you registered with us? ☐

USEFUL PHRASES

Clarifying and explaining
What do you mean exactly?
Sorry, what does that mean?
What exactly does OS stand for?
We just need to clarify a few things.
Could you explain what you've done so far?
Is that X or Y?
That means you need to ...
In other words, you have to ...
That's another word for X.

Checking comprehension
Can you find/see that all right?
Are you having any problems/trouble finding/seeing that?
Are you following me all right?
Is everything clear so far/up to this point?
Do you have any (other) questions so far/up to this point?

8 **Rearrange the words to make typical 'call centre' sentences. In each sentence there is one word that you don't need.**

1 just things need clarify a we few to must.

_____

2 anything so far clear everything is?

_____

3 far you done tell what could you've explain so?

_____

4 that to some means software you need mean install.

_____

5 does OS what for do stand?

_____

6 what do this I'm to when going is.

_____

7 me you just steps talk through the let us.

_____

CUSTOMER FOCUS EXTRA

Use 'signal' sounds and phrases to show you are listening carefully. It's important that the customer knows you are at the other end of the line and listening closely to what he or she is saying.

Use these phrases or words to show that you …
- are following what the customer is saying: *Uh uh./I see./Right./OK.*
- acknowledge the problem: *Really?/Is that so?*
- agree: *Uh uh./Of course.*

21

9 **Complete these extracts from call centre dialogues with a signal word or phrase. (C = customer / A = agent). Then listen to check your answers.**

C I left a message for the call centre manager to call me back. That was three days ago and I've heard nothing from him.

A _____[1] I'm so sorry. Let me see if I can help you …

C I've emailed your helpline three times, but the emails have all been returned.

A _____[2] I'm sorry about that. We must have had a problem with our server. It seems to be working all right now though. How can I help you?

C I'm having trouble with my television. It turns on and I can see the picture, but I can't seem to get any sound.

A _____[3]. OK, I'm going to need to ask you some questions …

C Your product is very good, but I'd like more information on an upgraded model.

A _____[4]. I think I can suggest something for you …

10   **Choose the best response to these call centre questions and requests.**

1   Can't you give me a better price for our first order?
   a   Sorry, I can't do that.
   b   Let me check with the manager and call you back in a few minutes.
   c   It might be possible.

2   Can you quote me a price?
   a   The price is a fair one.
   b   They cost 40 cents each.
   c   Our price is better than our competitors.

3   We are thinking of signing up for your service.
   a   Then why don't you take advantage of our introductory offer?
   b   Call us back when you've decided.
   c   I told you our prices yesterday.

4   Can you do a rush order for me?
   a   I'll try.
   b   Of course. This will go out by the end of the day.
   c   We can't process orders in a hurry, sorry.

5   I'd like to order five cases, please.
   a   OK, that's five cases.
   b   Are you sure you only want five?
   c   We have a special offer today: you get one case free when you order six.

6   When can the order be dispatched?
   a   Today, sir, in the overnight post.
   b   Maybe this evening.
   c   I'm not sure. We're having problems with our deliveries at the moment.

11   **Complete the puzzle with the noun form of the verbs below.**

Across
1   clarify
5   satisfy
6   explain
8   deliver

Down
2   assist
3   pay
4   offer
7   order

Now use words from above to complete the sentences.

a   Good. I'm glad I could help. Let me know if I can be of any more _____ .

b   I'll put you through to our IT specialist. She'll be able to give you a more detailed _____ and help solve the problem.

c   One of the best things about our introductory _____ is that you can take advantage of our new monthly _____ plan.

12   **Work with a partner to do a 'call centre' role-play. Either refer to the role cards in the partner files or think of your own situation.**

PARTNER FILES   Partner A   File 04, p. 58
Partner B   File 04, p. 60

Outlook

Read this article from a customer care website and answer the questions which follow.

Quote of the day
"Treat every customer as if they sign your paycheck, because they do."
Unknown

The Call Centre
Consultancy

Poor service is the fastest way to lose customers. Is your call centre doing everything possible to keep its customers happy?

- Home
- Services
- Training
- About us
- CCD help desk
- Contact us
- Feedback
- Links

Call centre experts tell us it costs 4 to 10 times as much to capture a new customer as it does to provide good service to an existing customer. A startling 68% of call centre customers move to the competition because of poor service.

Customer-centred call centres must look at their front lines – the agents. Their agents, after all, communicate with customers every day. This means that agents must have the right phone style and – for online help desks – appropriate email skills. The latter is even more important nowadays as emailing has become a record of promises kept – or broken – to customers.

Call centres can no longer afford to have agents who just read off scripts. Now agents need to be knowledge workers and salespeople for the complete range of customer service. For example, at the Hilton Hotels, agents don't just take reservations. If no rooms are available, the clerks try to cross-sell another of Hilton's six brands in the same city or area. This generates $250 million of revenue annually for the Hilton Hotels.

Click the calendar for call centre events

Free Newsletter Register now! Click here

At DHL Worldwide, call centres are focusing more on customer service and sales instead of just taking orders. A typical answer to "Do you ship to Manila?" is "Yes, with the fastest delivery time, 99% guaranteed." Call centre supervisors are now concerned with how well their agents sell DHL, not how quickly they get on and off the phone with customers.

NO, I'M SORRY – WE DON'T HAVE ANY OF THOSE BATHTUBS IN STOCK.

CAN I INTEREST YOU IN A SWIMMING POOL INSTEAD?

Over to you

Does your company have a call centre? If so, how can your call centre be more customer-centred? How can companies motivate their call centre agents to deliver more to their customers?

Key concept

Keep a customer-first attitude to manage the stress and demands of call centre work. Your positive attitude will affect your colleagues and customers!

Delivering customer care through writing

First approach

Do this quick quiz about writing for customer care. Say whether the statements are true (T) or false (F). Then compare your answers with a partner's.

1 The content of a letter or an email is more important than correct spelling and punctuation. ☐

2 It's always better to send an email than to phone a customer. ☐

3 You should always write to new customers in a formal style. ☐

4 If you can understand what you wrote in a letter, then your customer can too. ☐

5 If you have a spellchecker on your computer, you don't need to re-read letters or emails before sending them. ☐

6 Emails should normally be short and concise. ☐

7 If a customer's email or letter is informal, then your reply should also be informal. ☐

8 It's OK to send out form letters *[Serienbriefe]* to any customer enquiry. ☐

9 Customers appreciate smileys and other fun graphics in emails. ☐

1 Look at these excerpts from customer care letters and emails. Which one is …

1 an invitation? ☐

2 a follow-up to a meeting? ☐

3 a reply to an enquiry? ☐

4 a promise to send something? ☐

5 a request for information? ☐

a

Hello Mr Schmidt

In answer to your email, our shop in Essen is open Mondays through Saturdays from 9 am to 8 pm. You can reach us by fax on 0763 449 923.

Please feel free to get in touch if you have any more questions.

Regards
Lara Jones

b

Hi Oliver

We're having a small party at the Bavarian Hotel this Friday at 7 pm. We're asking a few of our most important clients to attend and I would be pleased if you could join us. Let me know if you can come …

Best wishes
Jochen

c

Dear Mrs Donath

Thanks so much for your phone call yesterday. I am pleased to tell you that we can handle your order. Would you like to pay by credit card or bank transfer? Please fill in the attached form and fax it to me. Then I can send it out to you today.

Best regards
Jeannette Donaldson

e   Robert

I got your message this afternoon. Sure, I'll talk to Ruth and email you the price list today. Do you also need our latest brochure?

Take care
Carola

d   Dear Mr Blair

In regard to our meeting yesterday, I would just like to confirm what we agreed. First of all, ...

Sincerely yours
Franz Wunderlich

Which of the above are from letters and which are from emails? How can you tell?

Which types of letters or emails do you write to your customers in English?

CUSTOMER FOCUS EXTRA

Salutations and closes

When you write to a customer for the first time, it is often best to use a formal style. Then look at how the customer answers. Is the reply formal or informal? From now on, use the same register as your customer. By communicating with the customer in the way he or she prefers, you demonstrate good customer care.

Here is an overview of standard salutations and closes used in letters and emails.

	letter	email
when you don't know the name	Dear Sir or Madam / Dear Sirs Ladies and Gentlemen (AE) —— Yours faithfully (BE) Sincerely (yours) (AE)	Dear Sir or Madam / Dear Sirs Hello —— (Kind / Best) Regards Best wishes
when you know the name	Dear Mr / Ms / Mrs Smith Dear Mr and Mrs Smith Dear Ms Black and Mr Smith —— Yours sincerely (BE) Sincerely (yours) (AE)	Dear / Hello Mr / Ms / Mrs Smith Dear / Hello Mr and Mrs Smith Dear / Hello Ms Black and Mr Smith —— (Kind/Best) Regards All the best / Best wishes
when you know the person / people well	Dear John Dear Paul and Mary —— Kind regards (With) best wishes	Dear / Hello / Hi John Hi Paul and Mary —— Best (wishes) / All the best Take care (AE) / Cheers (BE)

Note that in the US, the salutation in letters is often followed by a colon (Dear Mr Brown:). In the UK there is often no punctuation used here, but sometimes people put commas after *both* the salutation and the close (Dear John, ... Kind regards, ...). Whether there is a comma or not, the first word in letters and emails always starts with a capital letter.

2 **Which salutations and closes should you use when writing to the following people?**

informal

1   em@il → Hugo Jones
    Hi Hugo ... All the best
    _____

2   letter → Walter Rogers
    _____

3   letter → Mario Ingram & Janet Browne
    _____

formal

4   letter → Carol Elan
    _____

5   em@il → Jeanne & Pascal Duchard
    _____

6   letter → name unknown
    _____

3 **Read the letter and answer the questions.**

1   How well does Rüdiger know Mr Davis?
2   Where did they meet?
3   What did Mr Davis request?
4   What will happen next?

Find the English equivalents in the letter.

a   *Es hat mich gefreut ...*
b   *In der Anlage übersende ich Ihnen unseren neuesten Katalog ...*
c   *Ich melde mich am Donnerstag ...*
d   *Für weitere Fragen stehe ich gerne zur Verfügung.*
e   *Wie gewünscht ...*
f   *Es würde uns freuen, Sie als neuen und geschätzten Kunden begrüßen zu dürfen.*

Horizons International

Altstrasse 13 • 22609 Hamburg
Tel +49 40 654 372 • Fax +49 40 654 374 • Ruediger.Vogel@HorizInt.de

John Davis
Davis & Chapman Ltd
145 Cheltenham Rd
Bristol BS6 5QZ

Dear Mr Davis

It was a pleasure meeting you recently at the Business Executive Conference. I am delighted to be able to assist you in finding a suitable IT communications system for your company. As requested, I am enclosing our latest catalogue with details and prices.

I would be grateful if we could meet soon. I will phone you on Thursday and hope we can arrange a suitable date and time.

If you have any further questions, please do not hesitate to contact me.

I look forward to welcoming you as a new and valued customer.

Yours sincerely

Rüdiger Vogel

Rüdiger Vogel
Sales Manager

encl

4   **Match 1–6 with a–f to make phrases.**

1   I look forward to
2   We are delighted to
3   If you have
4   Thank you
5   It was a pleasure to
6   If you are satisfied
7   I will pay

a   for choosing our company
b   seeing you next week
c   you a visit personally
d   any further questions
e   speak to you
f   have you as a new customer
g   with the results

Now use the phrases to complete this email to a new customer.

Delete   Reply   Reply All   Forward   Print

From: "Verena Knull"
To: barbara.winston@gmax.de
Subject: telephone service

Dear Mrs Winston

_____ [1] on the phone

yesterday. _____

_____ [2]. As you requested, here is a summary of our discussion:

• You will receive monthly service for one year.

• _____ [3], you

   can renew your contract for as many years as you would like.

• Your service fees will be invoiced monthly.

• Finally, as you are a new customer, we can offer you a 10% introductory discount on your

   rate if you pay before the due date.

As we agreed, _____ [4]

next Thursday, 10 September, at 10.30 to show you how to start up the service.

_____ [5], please feel

free to contact me. Otherwise, _____

_____ [6] .

_____ [7].

Best regards

Verena Knull
Sales Manager

5   **Two versions of the same email – one formal and one informal – have been mixed up.**
Put them back in order.

Dear Mr Vogt
b _____
_____
_____
_____

Dear Manfred
_____
_____
_____
_____

a   In the meantime, if you have any other questions, please don't hesitate to contact me.
I look forward to seeing you next week.

b   In regard to your phone call this morning, I am writing to let you know about the latest developments.

c   I'm glad to tell you that we have found two new customers for you. It'd be great if we could set up a meeting at the end of next week to discuss this. Would you like me to email you the customer information today? You can review it before we meet.

d   Kind regards
J Hargreaves

e   Thanks for your phone call this morning. Just a quick email to let you know about the latest developments.

f   I am delighted to inform you that we have found two new customers for you. I would appreciate it if we could set up a meeting at the end of next week to discuss this. Would you like me to email you the customer information today? You can review it before we meet.

g   All the best
John

h   In the meantime, let me know if you need any other help.
Looking forward to seeing you next week.

6   Now find phrases in the two emails to complete the gaps in the box below.

FORMAL	INFORMAL
Connecting with the reader	
In reference to your letter/email of ...	Re your letter/email of ...
_____ 1	_____ 2
Further to our recent meeting ...	I hope everything is going well.
Reason for writing	
We are writing to confirm ...	I'm just writing to tell you ...
	I'd like to let you know ...
_____ 3	
I would like to inform you ...	_____ 4
Giving good news	
We are pleased to say ...	_____ 6
_____ 5	I'm happy to tell you ...
Requests	
We would be grateful if we could ...	_____ 8
_____ 7	Could you ... ?
Taking action	
I will phone you/contact you ...	I'll get in touch with/get back to you ...
We would be delighted/pleased to assist you.	I'd be glad to help out.
Concluding	
Please feel free to contact me/us if you have any further questions.	Let me know if you need anything else.
_____ 9	_____ 11
We look forward to hearing from/meeting you soon.	Looking forward to your reply/to hearing from you.
_____ 10	_____ 12

7   Complete these sentences from letters and emails with the missing words.

back • convenience • hearing • just • of • pleased • regard • reply • would

1   In _____ to your phone call, I am sending you the specifications for model XRT32.

2   We would be _____ to assist you with all your financial planning.

3   Thanks for your letter _____ 29 June.

4   I'll get _____ to you as soon as possible.

5   We look forward to _____ from you soon.

6   I _____ be grateful if you could contact me at your earliest _____ .

7   Looking forward to your _____ .

8   I'm _____ writing to let you know the dates of our next open house.

CUSTOMER FOCUS EXTRA

Follow the five Cs of customer care writing to make sure your writing is:

clear Keep sentences short and direct, and have well organized paragraphs.

complete Include all the information your customer needs, including reference numbers and contact details.

concise Don't waste your reader's time with too much extra information. Remember your customer is also a busy person!

courteous and Use polite language and follow letter-writing conventions.

correct Don't distract the reader with mistakes in grammar, punctuation and spelling. Always re-read your letter or email before sending it!

---

8 **First study the tips in the box above and say what is wrong with this email. Which of the five Cs has the writer ignored? Then rewrite the email.**

An: Mira Jones <m_jones@ts_enterprises.com>
Betreff: select systems price list

Dear Mira Jones

It was a plasure to meet you recently at the Global Concepts trade fair. Our exhibit areas were on the second floor of the Bellevue Hotel. I hope you enjoyed the fair as much as I did. How did you like the food at our VIP customer lunch? I wish they had served us chicken, not beef. After all the worries about BSE, I don't like beef much anymore.

I want to phone you at the end of the week to arrange an appointment to meet you so we can discuss your customer needs. Is Friday afternoon suitable for you I'm busy all Friday morning, but think I have time on Friday afternoon, perhaps at around 2 pm. What do you think? Would that be okay.

Thanks you for your intrest in Select Systems GmbH. I look forward to speak to you soon.

Here is the price list you asked for. Do you still want me to send you our catalogue? If so, confirm your postal address.

Best regards

22–24

9 **Listen to the voicemail messages. Then match these written responses (a–c) to the messages (1–3). Which responses are from emails and which are from letters? How can you tell?**

a ☐ Thank you for your phone call of 2 May. I'm sorry we were not available to take your call.
Please find attached a brochure about our services. You can also visit us online at www.bestfoods.de for more detailed information.
If you have any other questions, please do not hesitate to contact us.

b ☐ Sorry we weren't in when you called.
I've attached a pdf of the specifications for model 830T.
Should I also arrange to send you some product brochures
for the shop?
Let me know if you need anything else.

c ☐ Thank you for your reservation of 2 May.
I'd like to confirm the following:
1 single room with a bath for two nights from 5 to 7 May.
As you requested, we have enclosed a magazine listing all events taking place in May.
Please feel free to contact us if you require any assistance with bookings.
We look forward to welcoming you to our hotel.

CUSTOMER FOCUS EXTRA

Make sure you review your documents carefully before sending them to the customer. Like the letter or email message itself, you need to view it through the customer's eyes. Is it appropriate? Does it present a positive image? Take an extra moment to check the enclosures or attachments before you close the envelope or hit the send button!

You can use the following language to refer to the enclosed or attached documents:

letter	**email**
Please find enclosed/I am enclosing the price list you requested.	*I'm sending you the current price list as an attachment.*
	I've attached the specifications as a pdf document.
In the enclosed information packet, you will find product descriptions, ...	*Please complete the attached form and return it ...*
	Please find attached ...
As you will see from the enclosed brochure, ...	*Here is the file you asked for.* (informal)

---

10 **Use the phrases from page 43 and above to write a customer-friendly reply to the following email enquiry.**

> An: Just-in-Berlin Relocation Centre <info@just-in-berlin.com>
> Von: Joan White <jwhite@quickmail.com>
>
> Hello
>
> I have just visited your website about relocation services. I will soon be moving to Berlin so am looking for an agency to help me find a flat. Can you also recommend a place to lease a car for my business?
>
> I was not able to find any information about your prices on your website, so could you please send me a current price list? Also, I will be in Berlin at the end of the month – could we perhaps set up a meeting? My mobile number is 0188 59773.
>
> Thank you for your assistance. I look forward to hearing from you and hopefully meeting you soon.
>
> Regards
> Joan White
>
> White Associates
> jwhite@quickmail.com

Don't forget to:

use a formal salutation and close
connect with reader
give a reason for writing
offer help
take action
end the email politely

11 Work with a partner to practise writing emails and letters. Either think of your own situation or look at the ones in the partner files. Try to use phrases from this unit.

PARTNER FILES
Partner A   File 05, p. 59
Partner B   File 05, p. 61

Outlook

Read this case study about customer care provided via the Internet and answer the questions.

Giving customers 'the no-answer runaround' –

A CASE STUDY

Customers have become used to the speedy response or quick 'turn-around time' of Internet exchange and are therefore sometimes more demanding and less patient than they used to be. They want quick answers to their service questions. Here is a typical customer experience and its result.

A customer asked a large catalogue store whether a hand-held computer he was planning to buy from their company could be used for PowerPoint presentations. The response was: 'Visit our website under FAQ' (the common abbreviation for 'Frequently Asked Questions'). When the customer looked at the FAQs, he could not find the right question for his problem. His 'search' attempt got no answers either, so he wrote his question in the 'other enquiries' field.

The customer got this answer immediately: 'Thank you for your email. We will try to handle your request as soon as possible. Since we get so many enquiries, it is faster to refer to the FAQ section or use the search tools to find your answer.'

The customer was back at the beginning.

The frustrated customer finally gave up and changed to another brand of palm computers. When he emailed the new company's service centre, he got a direct answer with efficiency and courtesy. He was so pleased with the quick and polite service that he recommended the hand-held computer to several of his colleagues.

Over to you

Share a personal experience with a partner about dealing with automated online customer care. How did it make a positive or negative impression on you?

Describe ways a customer service centre can be sure that an automated system gives customers the help they need.

Does your company have a website offering customer service? If so, how is it set up? What kind of FAQs do you have? How do you deal with enquiries sent via the website?

Key concept

People expect *efficiency* from customer care. Your direct and clear communication in writing should waste neither your customer's time – nor yours!

6

Dealing with problems and complaints

First approach

Look at this list of things that customers complain about. Which three things annoy you the most as a customer? Compare your answers with a partner's.

a Being put on hold when you call somebody

b Getting an engaged signal when trying to call

c Being transferred many times when you call

d Unhelpful staff

e Salespeople with little or no knowledge of their products and services

f Not enough staff to help customers

g Receiving too much junk mail or advertising

h Getting complicated, unclear explanations

i Not getting quick answers to emails

Can you add anything else to the list? How can companies avoid annoying their customers?

1 **Read this email from a customer service manager to her staff. Work with a partner to write an action checklist for the meeting.**

Hello everyone,

Recently we have been getting a lot of complaints from customers who are annoyed with the quality of our customer service. Here are just three of the comments we've received:

"I had a problem with one of your products. When I told the salesperson about it, he was arrogant and acted like my problem was stupid and unimportant. He even suggested that the problem was my fault."

"The person on the phone didn't even listen to what I was saying. I had to repeat myself two or three times. Then she just said, 'Well, that's our company policy. I can't do anything about it.' She didn't even apologize!"

"I realize I was angry and perhaps spoke sharply, but the agent didn't have to yell at me. He told me it wasn't his fault and that I should speak to the person who made the mistake, not him."

At our next staff meeting, I want to discuss our complaints policy and how we can improve our customer care. I would like you all to make an action checklist on how to improve the way we handle customers, and present your ideas at the meeting.

1 selected

VOCABULARY ASSISTANT

annoyed *verärgert*   company policy *Firmenpolitik*
to realize sth *sich klar über etw sein/werden*
sharply *gereizt*   to yell at sb *jdn anschreien*

2 Here are some of the ideas presented at the meeting. Work with a colleague to decide whether they belong to the do or don't list.

do	don't
_____	_____
_____	_____
_____	_____

1   Let the customers show their anger.
2   Say the problem was the customer's fault.
3   Tell the customer there's nothing you can do.
4   Listen carefully to the details of the problem.
5   Push the customer to accept your point of view.
6   Take the customer's anger as a personal criticism.
7   Offer a more expensive product or service to replace the first order.
8   Summarize and make sure the customer agrees to the plan of action.

3 Three customers are making complaints. Listen and match the dialogues to the pictures. Then complete the table.

25–27

a

b

NEXT TELLER PLEASE

c

	complaint	response
Dialogue 1	_____	_____
Dialogue 2	_____	_____
Dialogue 3	_____	_____

VOCABULARY ASSISTANT

to inconvenience sb *jdm Umstände machen*
interruptions *Unterbrechungen*   receipt *Beleg*
to refund *(zurück)erstatten*   teller *(Bank-)Kassierer/in*

4 **Listen again and complete these sentences from the dialogues.**

25–27

Dialogue 1   1 I'm _____ to _____ that.

2 What _____ to be the _____ ?

3 First of all, _____ for the poor service …

Dialogue 2   4 I _____ the stress you must be feeling …

5 I'm sorry that you've been so _____.

6 So, _____ how I can _____ you.

Dialogue 3   7 It _____ that our shop assistant made a _____.

8 I'll be happy to _____ your money.

9 That's no _____. I'll _____ to help you.

CUSTOMER FOCUS EXTRA

In problems and complaints we often soften bad news by using phrases such as
I'm afraid (that) we've made a mistake.
It seems (that) there has been a mix-up with your order.
It appears (that) they forgot to enclose the instructions.
There seems/appears to be a misunderstanding.

We can also combine these phrases with the passive tense to acknowledge the
problem without saying who exactly made the mistake.
It seems/appears (that) the order **was not handled** promptly enough.
I'm afraid (that) a mistake **has been made**.

---

5 **Write a customer-friendly statement for each situation using the phrases in the box above.**

1 You're wrong. Our information is right, not yours. (seems/misunderstanding)

   There seems to be a misunderstanding.

2 It wasn't my colleague's fault that you didn't get the order. (afraid/mix-up)

   _____

3 The agent didn't put some of the parts in the shipment. (appears/include)

   _____

4 I didn't get your email, so it's obvious that you didn't send it. (seems/get though)

   _____

5 You won't get the order this week. (afraid/delay)

   _____

6 That's a mistake, but it's your fault, not mine. (appears/mistake)

   _____

6   **What's wrong with the following answers to a customer's complaint? How do you think the customer would react in each case?**

1   "I don't really deal with that. That's not my department."
2   "Well, I've never done that before but I'll try it and see what happens."
3   "We can't help you with that. We don't carry that product here."
4   "I don't know."
5   "We don't give refunds – as soon as you leave the store, it's yours."

Here are some more effective answers to complaints. Match 1–5 from above with a–e below.

a   We have an exchange policy, but I'm afraid we don't give refunds. So, please make your selection carefully before buying. Could I help you decide which product is the best for you?
b   I could give you some general advice, but it's better if you speak to my colleague. He is the specialist in this area. May I transfer you to him?
c   I'm really not certain about that, but I'll find out for you. I'll ring you back by 4 pm today. Is that OK?
d   I'm afraid this isn't something we carry. I can recommend that you contact T&C. I'm sure that they carry that product.
e   That sounds like something we could do for you, but I need to make sure. May I ask my manager about it and call you back?

28

7   **Read this dialogue about a problem-solving situation in a hotel and complete the gaps with phrases from the list. Then listen to check your answers.**

> Excuse me • I can see how • I'd be glad • I'd like to say • inconvenienced •
> make sure • seems to be • straight away • understand • Would you mind

Guest	_____[1], I have a complaint about your hotel.
Receptionist	Oh, you look very troubled. What _____[2] the problem, madam?
Guest	Well, we're regular guests at your hotel, but I'm about to change my mind about ever staying here again! The service is terrible. I've had to ring housekeeping every day to ask them to clean my room. My company pays good rates for me and my colleagues to stay at your hotel, so a dependable cleaning service is the least we expect!
Receptionist	First of all, _____[3] how sorry I am. _____[4] this must have ruined your stay with us. So, if I _____[5] you correctly, you had to phone each day to get your room serviced?
Guest	That's right.
Receptionist	_____[6] giving me some details? If I could just have your name and your room number and what time you called and who you spoke to exactly …

• • •

Receptionist   Ms Jones, I'll speak to housekeeping

_____ [7]. I want to

_____ [8] this never

happens again. Since you've been so

_____ [9] by this incident,

_____ [10] to offer you

two free nights for your next visit at our

hotel. In fact, I'll give you a voucher right

now. You can use it any time you wish.

Guest   Oh, that's just great! I am so glad that we

could work this out. We do want to keep

coming back here.

VOCABULARY ASSISTANT	incident *Zwischenfall* troubled *besorgt* voucher *Gutschein*

8   How did the hotel receptionist deal with the problem? First complete the statements with the correct form of the verbs from the list. Then write down the phrases she used.

apologize • ask for • ~~listen~~ • offer • repeat • take

What the receptionist did:	What the receptionist said:
1 She _listened_ to the guest carefully.	–
2 She _____ after hearing the guest's story.	_____ _____
3 She _____ the problem back to the guest.	_____ _____
4 She _____ more information about the problem.	_____ _____
5 She _____ action to help the guest straight away.	_____ _____
6 She _____ compensation for the guest's trouble.	_____ _____

CUSTOMER FOCUS EXTRA

We don't want customers complaining over and over again about the same problems.
Make sure you ask for as many details as possible to deal with every complaint effectively.
Show the customer your intention to take care of the whole problem, not just bits and
pieces. This is the key to customer satisfaction for today – and for the future.

9   **Look at the problem-solving flow chart below and match the headings to the phrases.**

a   Clarify the information and repeat the problem back to the customer.
b   End with a friendly, helpful tone.
c   Assure the client of follow-up.
d   Apologize.
e   Summarize the discussion.
f   Offer an alternative if the customer doesn't accept the solution.
g   Listen carefully to the customer describe the problem and show empathy.
h   Say how and when the problem will be solved.
i   Take responsibility for the problem.

> **VOCABULARY ASSISTANT**
>
> to assure *zusichern*
> empathy *Mitgefühl*
> oversight *Versehen*
> to resolve *klären*
> to solve *lösen*

1
First of all, I'm so / terribly sorry about that.
I apologize for ...
Let me apologize for ...

2
Could you tell me exactly what happened?
Could you explain a bit more ... ?
Do you mind if I just go over that again ... ?

3
I'll just make a few notes as you speak.
I understand. / I see what you mean.
I would feel the same way.
What a difficult situation this puts you in.

4
It looks like an oversight on our part.
There seems to be a misunderstanding.
It appears your order got overlooked.
I'm afraid there has been some sort of mix-up.

5
I'll take care of this at once for you.
I'm sure we can find a solution.
I'd be glad to offer you ... to make up for this inconvenience.
This should be resolved by the end of today.

6
If this solution does not meet your needs, then I can suggest ... as an alternative.
I'll look into other possibilities by ...
I'll get back to you straight away.
You'll receive (a refund / replacement) by tomorrow ...

7
What we have decided is ...
Our action plan is ...
I'd like to go over this once more to make sure we agree.

8
I'll get back to you ...
I'll follow up to make sure that ...

9
I hope you are satisfied with the outcome.
Thanks for bringing this to our attention.
Is there anything else I can help you with today?
Don't hesitate to ring again if there are any more problems.

10 Work with a partner. Choose one of the situations below (or think of a situation of your own) and use information in the partner files to do a face-to-face or telephone role-play. Note that Partner A is always the customer. Make sure you follow the steps for problem-solving.

Situation 1   A damaged consignment and a mistake on an invoice
Situation 2   A noisy hotel room on a business trip

PARTNER FILES   Partner A   File 06, p. 59
Partner B   File 06, p. 61

11 Read this typical letter of apology and complete the gaps with the phrases below.

> We very much regret

> We are very concerned to hear

> Once again, we apologize

> We assure you that we are doing everything we can

> The problem has now been resolved

Dear Mr Weber

_____[1] that your order from last month
has not reached you. _____[2] the
frustration this has caused you.

_____[3] to make sure your
order arrives as soon as possible. The delay was due to an unexpected computer
problem in the delivery department which interrupted our usual efficient service.
_____[4] and your order
has been sent to you by overnight post.

_____[5] for the inconvenience. We do
value your business and hope to keep you as a long-term customer.

Yours sincerely

Mark Becker

Dispatch Manager

Find phrases in the letter above. How did Mark Becker ...

a state the problem?
b apologize to the customer?
c show empathy with the customer?

d explain the reason for the problem?
e offer a solution?

12   **We sometimes have to explain our company policy when responding to complaints.**
Match the policy with a customer-friendly way to explain it.

policy

1   We don't give estimates out on the phone.
2   We don't ship by regular post, only by overnight express.
3   We don't send out our diet products unless the customer has been checked by a doctor.
4   We block any credit card charge that looks unusual or has a high amount.
5   We can't do anything about our bank service charges.

explanation

a   This ensures the safe use of our products.
b   We aim to give the highest standards in managing your bank accounts.
c   This helps us give you a fairer and more accurate quote.
d   This ensures that your food products arrive fresh.
e   This is a security precaution to make sure your card has not been stolen.

VOCABULARY ASSISTANT	accurate *genau* to ensure that *dafür sorgen, dass …*
	estimate *Kostenvoranschlag* quote *Kostenvoranschlag*
	security precaution *Sicherheitsvorkehrung*

Can you add another example of your own company policy?
How can you say it in a polite, positive way so that the customer understands and accepts it?

13   **Work with a partner. You both work for Darstein Communications and have received the following**
three complaints. First discuss how to deal with them: by telephone, in person or in writing.
Then choose one complaint and decide how to respond.

1

I'm writing to you because I've been trying to get through to your helpline for the past three days. I've called several times during the day and night, but have never got through, not even once! I'm trying to enquire about something on my monthly bill. It's useless to have a helpline if it is always busy! I plan to visit your manager next week to discuss this in person.

1 selected

2

I became a subscriber to your service because you promised six months of cheap phone calls to the UK, which is where my brother lives right now. When I got your invoice though, I was completely shocked to see that the UK phone calls are twice as expensive as before, with my old phone service. What happened to the low, low rates?! I find this misleading advertising totally unacceptable.

3

As a regular customer of yours for nearly five years now, I find this latest incident with your call centre totally unacceptable. I phoned in recently to enquire about the latest service upgrades. The agent informed me that I could not add any other features to my IT system. I only bought the system from you six months ago. The agent told me someone had sold me a 'limited system', so no action could be taken. Then, I asked to speak to her supervisor, so she put me on hold. To my dismay, I got disconnected. I tried to ring back, but again got an engaged signal.

VOCABULARY ASSISTANT

misleading *irreführend*   subscriber *Abonnent/in*
supervisor *Vorgesetzte/r*   to my dismay *zu meiner*

Outlook

Look at what these people say about customer complaints and apologies. Do any of the comments sound familiar?

I lived in England for a while and was impressed with how easily the words 'I'm sorry' can help defuse a difficult situation. A lot of my colleagues here in Germany prefer not to say it when dealing with complaints because they say: 'The problem's not my fault, why should I apologize?' But I just think it means: 'I'm sorry about the situation and want to help you'. It doesn't mean that I'm responsible.

We get a lot of complaints online to our website and it's amazing how rude and insulting some customers can be. Perhaps it's because they think they're not talking to a real person, just a machine. But real people like me read the messages and then have to answer in a friendly and professional manner. Sometimes it's quite difficult to do so and I wonder what these customers would think if I wrote the same type of angry messages to them!

I'm a Canadian living in Germany and I must admit it's taken me a long time to get used to customer service here. I used to be very polite when I complained about a product or service in a shop, for example. I said 'please' and 'bitte' and smiled a lot, and the shop assistants just looked at me like I was crazy! I don't think they took me seriously. Now when I have a complaint, I don't smile. I'm very direct and just state my problem. And I get a much better response from the shop assistants this way. Perhaps it's just a cultural thing.

Over to you

How do you deal with complaints at your company or business ? Is it the same or different than other companies you know or do business with?
How do people in similar jobs in other countries deal with complaints? Do you think there are cultural differences in the way customers complain and what they complain about? How about the way apologies are made?

Key concept

Problems and complaints help us make our customer care more focused and realistic. If our customers are silent, then how will we ever know how to improve?

Test yourself!

See how much you have learned about customer care. Use the clues to complete the crossword puzzle.

Across

3   Another word for 'to seem': *It ... that we made a mistake.*

4   It's always important to show good listening skills or to be ... to customers.

6   When you don't understand the customer, you can say '*Sorry, I didn't quite ... that. Could you say it again?*

8   Another way to say 'I handle customer orders': *I'm ... for customer orders.*

9   Another way to say 'to phone' or 'to call': *Can I ... you back tomorrow?*

16   A way to offer further assistance: *Can I help you with ... ... today?* (2 words)

19   Another word for 'help': *How can I ... you?*

20   Another word for 'pleased': *I'd be ... to have you as a new customer.*

21   To give bad news to a customer, you can say: *I'm ... that we can't send out the software today.*

22   A way to show follow-up: *I'll ... ... she calls you back today.* (2 words)

24   If you want to make sure an address is correct, you can say: *I'd like to ... your address.*

25   When you want to check information with the customer, you can say: *May I ... ... that once again?* (2 words)

26   A way to end a letter or email: *I look ... to hearing from you.*

27   Something to say at the end of a letter: *If you have any questions, please don't ... to contact me.*

Down

1   A way to end a phone call: *Thank you. We ... your business.*

2   Something you want to build or establish with customers: a good ...

5   Showing ... means you understand what the customer is feeling.

6   When you want to set up a meeting, you might say: *Would Tuesday be ... for you?*

7   A customer at a trade fair who doesn't want help might say: *No, thank you. I'm just ... .*

10   Another way to say 'immediately': *I'll send you the package ... .* (2 words)

11   When you want to check that everybody understands something, you can say: *We just need to ... a few things.*

12   A way to check that the customer is happy with your service: *I hope this is to your ... .*

13   A way to start a presentation at a trade fair: *I'd like to ... you here today.*

14   Another phrase to say 'I'm sorry': *I'd like to ... for the delay.*

15   When you meet someone for the first time, you can say: *I'd like to ... myself.*

17   We often start a meeting or phone call with ... ... to make customers feel comfortable. (2 words)

18   To see if something is OK, you can say: *Would you ... if I phoned you tomorrow?*

23   A formal close in email writing: *Kind ...*

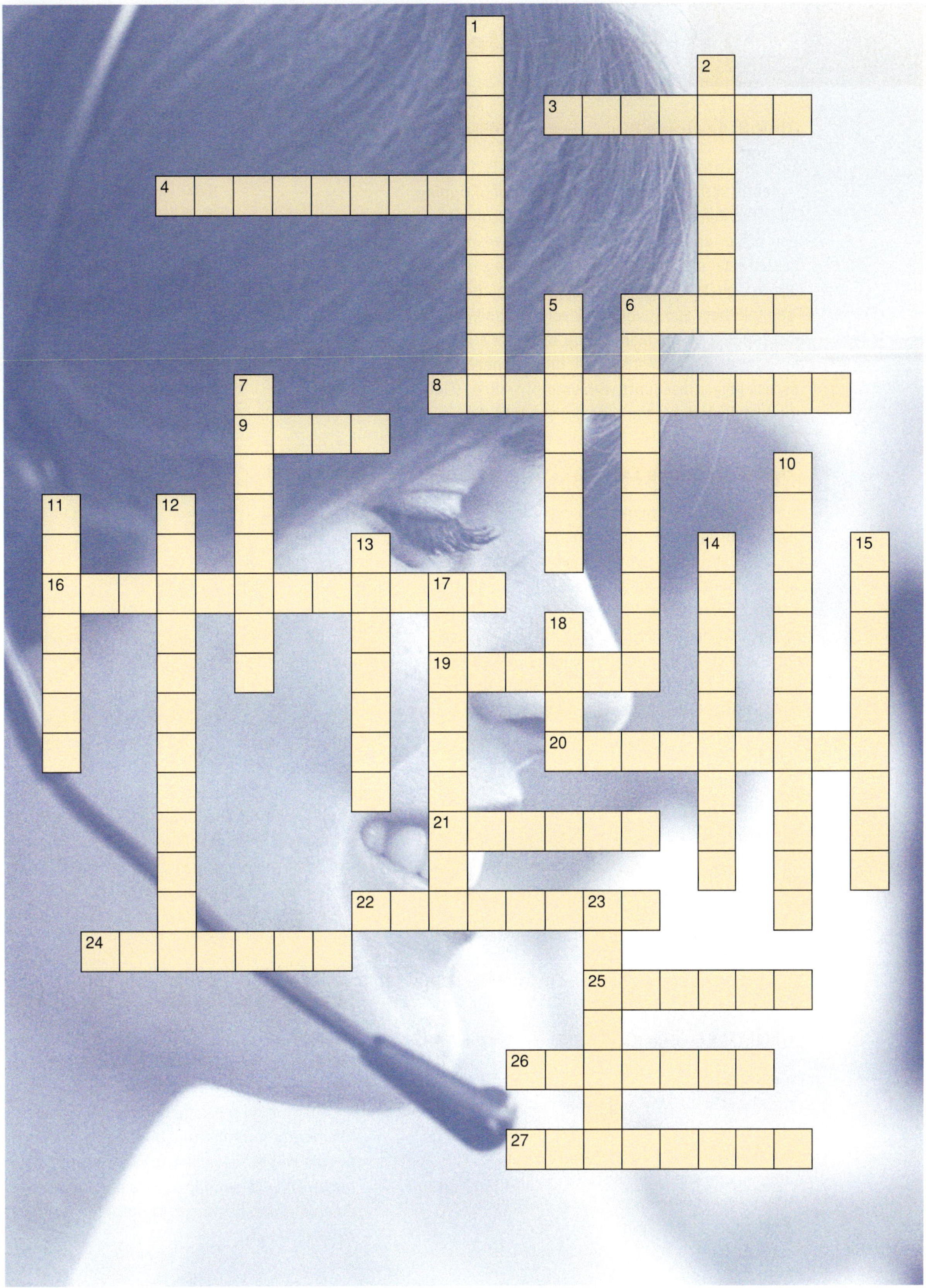
1
2
3
4
5
6
7
8
9
10
11
12
13
14
15
16
17
18
19
20
21
22
23
24
25
26
27

Unit 2, Exercise 9   File 01

You work in the sales department of NeuTech IT. Someone in the marketing department of Shopping Unlimited Retailers UK has asked you to come to their offices and tell them about your new software for customer mailing lists. After greetings and small talk, ask questions to get to know the company. Then tell them about your new software: it's the best product on the market. You can offer a 25% discount on your latest system, but you need to discuss bigger discounts with your boss first. (Only good customers get the bigger discount.)

Unit 2, Exercise 14   File 02

You're the assistant marketing director for HealthyLife Assurance in the UK. You're working at the stand at a trade fair when you see a potential customer. Introduce yourself and offer assistance. Unfortunately you don't have any more brochures (today is the last day of the fair) but you can send some when you are back in the office. Take the customer's contact details and ask about the best way to get in touch (by email? a visit?).

HealthyLife Assurance

D.T. Kennison
Assistant Marketing Director

7 Garrison Road
Manchester M15 4BX
UK
++ 44 161 8720767
DTKennison@healthylife.com
www.healthylife.co.uk

Unit 3, Exercise 12   File 03

Phone call 1
Today is Friday, 2 May. You are in London until Wednesday next week and would like to visit Gillian Browne in her office there. (You met at a recent trade fair and she is interested in your products.) If she's not there when you call, ask to speak to someone else that can help.

MAI	KW 18
5 Montag	9.00 M. Brooks 11.30 Tramten 15.15 Meet JT on Bond St
6 Dienstag	9.30 JT
7 Mittwoch	13.00 meet T&R for lunch Meeting 14.30 (Sara 16.00?) 20.30 BA456 Heathrow
8 Donnerstag	11.30 Hr Thiele
9 Freitag	

Phone call 2
You are the manager of the Italian ski resort Sci per Tutti. You wrote an email to ProfiSport yesterday asking for information about their latest ski equipment (catalogue and price list), and now somebody from the company is calling you to arrange a meeting. You are very busy next week but will be at the resort every day except Tuesday afternoon and Friday morning. (You might also have a lunch appointment on Thursday but are not 100% sure.)

Unit 4, Exercise 12   File 04

Situation 1
You work in the call centre at WeltReise GmbH. You receive a call from a customer who would like information on package holidays to Japan. Ask him/her for information about dates, how many people will be travelling, and the customer's price range. Offer to send the customer your catalogue by email or post. Be sure to confirm the customer's contact details.

Situation 2

You work at a department store and you deal with customer information. You need information from your customer files in order to write a report. You can open the files, but unfortunately the text is scrambled and you can't read the information. You need to adjust the text setting, but you don't know how. Call your IT support agent to help you solve this problem.

> Call IT dept!
> Can enter password and open customer files but can't read the text – scrambled!
> Tried 'new start' twice but still same problem.
> How do I adjust the text setting?

Unit 5, Exercise 11   File 05

Write an email.

At a recent trade fair you met a new customer who is interested in information about your latest laptop. He/She gave you his/her business card and you promised to send the new brochure straight away. (You also saw him/her later at one of the trade fair cafés and had a quick lunch together.) Write your follow-up email (remember to attach the information he/she asked for) and give it to Partner B.

```
                              R. Heck
        TGT GmbH
        _____

                      Liebigstr. 387
                      50935 Köln
                      RHeck@tgt.com
                      www.tgt.com
```

Respond to an email.

Your name is F. Ramos and you are the customer service manager at Siniad AG. You are arranging a seminar for 25 of your call centre agents and have called a hotel near your offices to find out about the menu and prices for a buffet lunch and coffee breaks. You now receive an email from the hotel (Partner B). Write an email back thanking Partner B for the information. You will try to make a decision by next week.

Unit 6, Exercise 10   File 06

Situation 1 (phone call)

You are calling RFH Catering Supplies to complain about a problem with your order. You've been charged double for the shipping fee on the last order of beer glasses and some of the glasses were also damaged during shipment. You've got a big party to service tomorrow, so you want RFH Catering to send the glasses straight away (it's urgent!) and to correct the invoice.

Invoice	*27 damaged* *35 damaged*		
Contents	**Cat no.**	**Unit Price**	**Total**
100 beer glasses	VG3982	.62	62.00
100 wine glasses	WG7632	.75	75.00
100 wine glasses	WG6723	.81	81.00
200 small plates	RS6781	.55	110.00
		Subtotal	328.00
		Shipping	44.00
should be € 22		Total	372.00

Situation 2 (face to face)

You are a guest at the Hotel Majestic and go to the hotel office to speak to the manager. You want to complain that your room is too noisy. The people in the next room have loud parties every night and you've not been able to sleep very well, so you're tired for your business meetings. Also, the hotel bed is very uncomfortable which makes it even more difficult to get some rest. Tell the manager to take action or you will move to another hotel.

Unit 2, Exercise 9 — File 01

You work in the marketing department at Shopping Unlimited Retailers UK and have asked someone from the sales department of NeuTech IT to visit your company and tell you about their new software package for customer mailing lists. First greet the visitor and offer hospitality. Introduce him or her to any colleagues at the meeting and make small talk for 2 or 3 minutes before talking business. Be prepared to answer questions about your company. You are very interested in the software but you expect a 40% discount. You have another meeting to go to, but you want him or her to contact you tomorrow with an offer.

Unit 2, Exercise 14 — File 02

You are the personnel manager of Sonnenschein GmbH, a company based in Munich. You are at a trade fair to find out about employee benefits, and especially life assurance programmes, for your staff in the UK branch of your company. You are not ready to buy anything yet. You just want information (perhaps some brochures?) to take back to your office. (Unfortunately you only have one business card with you – it's the last day of the fair – and you don't want to give it away.)

Sonnenschein GmbH

Waldstrasse 23
81679 München
Tel 089 77334709
Fax 089 77334719

S Ruft
Personnel Manager   S.Ruft@sonnenschein.de

Unit 3, Exercise 12 — File 03

Phone call 1
Today is Friday 2 May. Your colleague – Gillian Browne – is not in the office today. But she has given you her diary and asked you to make appointments for her.

Week of 5 May

Monday	4 pm dept meeting
Tuesday	8 am breakfast meeting (until 10?) Meet Zak at 5 pm
Wednesday	John & Paulo – 10.30 (+ lunch?) pm Work on presentation (no calls)
Thursday	Annual meeting, Stockholm flight 8.30 am
Friday	return flight 5.15 pm

Phone call 2
You are a sales rep for ProfiSport, a company which sells sports equipment. The manager of the Italian ski resort Sci per Tutti emailed you yesterday and asked for a price list and catalogue for your latest ski equipment. Call her or him to say that you will send the information straight away. You will also be in the area at the end of next week and could visit on Thursday, if that's convenient. Perhaps you could take him/her out for lunch.

Unit 4, Exercise 12 — File 04

Situation 1
Your name is P. Richardson and you are a regular customer with WeltReise GmbH. You phone their call centre (ask for somebody who speaks English!) to get information on package holidays to Japan. You'd like to go in September for 10 days with two friends and you don't want to pay more than ca €2,500 per person. You need the information quickly, so confirm your email address with the call centre agent.

Situation 2

You are an IT support agent for a call centre. You get a call from someone at a department store who is having trouble reading the customer information files. Ask him/her to explain how and when the problem happens. Then use the troubleshooting checklist to tell the person what to do. Make sure the customer follows and understands the steps. If the customer still can't read the files, offer to send a service technician at a convenient time.

Troubleshooting checklist

Problem:	*can't read files/scrambled text*
Action steps:	*click on 'format', then on 'text read'*
	click on 'text align' and press 'enter'
	it should be possible to read text now
Problem:	*has forgotten password*
Action steps:	

Unit 5, Exercise 11   File 05

Write an email.

You work at the Palast Hotel and one of your responsibilities is to arrange conferences and company events. You spoke to a new customer on the phone yesterday and want to write an email now to confirm what you agreed. He/she is planning a seminar at their offices (which are near your hotel) and wants to arrange a buffet lunch and two coffee breaks for 25 call centre agents. You told the customer that you will email him/her a menu and other information, including a price list. Write the email and give it to Partner A.

F. Ramos (f.ramos@siniadcorp.de)

Customer service manager, Siniad AG

Seminar for call centre agents – 25 people

lunch & 2 coffee breaks,
   21 September 1pm

email menu and price list (pdf files)

Respond to an email.

Your name is R Heck and you work at a company called BizNet GmbH in Cologne. You were at a trade fair recently and asked different people to send you information about their products. You have just received an email from one of the people you met there (Partner A). Write a response.

Unit 6, Exercise 10   File 06

Situation 1 (phone call)

You're the order agent for RFH Catering Supplies and a customer calls you to complain. Ask for details to solve the problem. Tell the customer that you will correct the invoice and then send him/her the new glasses by 5 pm today. Offer the customer a discount on the next order of glasses.

Invoice

Contents	Cat no.	Unit Price	Total
100 beer glasses	VG3982	.62	62.00
100 wine glasses	WG7632	.75	75.00
100 wine glasses	WG6732	.81	81.00
200 small plates	RS6781	.55	110.00
		Subtotal	328.00
		Shipping	44.00
		Total	372.00

Situation 2 (face to face)

You are the manager of Hotel Majestic and a guest comes to your office to complain. Note that your hotel is usually very quiet and suitable for business people, but this week there is a tennis tournament going on in your town and the hotel is full of younger people, who are unfortunately quite noisy. Give the guest something extra for his/her trouble such as free drinks, dinner or a voucher for a free room for his/her next stay.

Answer key

UNIT 1

page 5

1 customer satisfaction
customer convenience
customer-friendly
customer aim

(model answer)
1 *updated technology*
2 convenient website
3 helps customers choose right product
4 efficient service
5 positive image

page 6

2
1	to boast of	a	priority
2	priority	b	assist
3	to recommend	c	essential
4	to assist	d	convenient
5	efficient	e	efficient
6	convenient	f	recommend
7	enjoyable		
8	essential		

3 (model answers)
1 top quality products/goods and service
2 our good/competitive prices
3 free delivery and set-up/assembly/our online service/24-hour service
4 taking care of any customer problem within 48 hours
5 keep our customers coming back

page 7

4
1 receptionist
2 sales
3 representative
4 order entry clerk
5 shop assistant
6 cashier
7 teller
8 hotel
9 concierge
10 restaurant

5 (model answers)
1 A receptionist/A cashier/A shop assistant/A teller
2 A sales representative/A waiter/A shop assistant
3 An agent/A concierge/A bank officer/A teller
4 A sales manager/An agent
5 An order entry clerk/An agent/A sales representative
6 An agent/A manager/An officer

page 8

6 (model answers)
good telephone manner
good communication skills

ability to work well with customers/good customer service skills
ability to deal with complaints and problems
team work/ability to work in a team
being polite and diplomatic

7
1	N	5	N
2	P	6	N
3	N	7	P
4	P	8	P

page 9

8
1	*to be attentive*	5	prompt
2	to be in a hurry	6	impatient
3	rude	7	helpful
4	well informed	8	special

a attentive/patient/helpful/well informed/prompt
b rude
c uninformed/rude/impatient/unhelpful
d well informed
e rude/unhelpful/uninformed; well informed/polite/helpful

page 10

Outlook
1 D　　2 D　　3 A　　4 D

UNIT 2

page 11

1 (model answers)

1	N	5	P
2	P	6	P
3	N	7	N
4	N		

page 12

2
1 a bank
2 a shop
3 a hotel
4 a company
5 a trade fair

1 How are you today?
2 let me know
3 Could you
4 May
5 meet you

a 5
b 1
c 2, 4
d 3

3
1 must be
2 introduce
3 Nice

4 How was
5 May I take
6 you'd like
7 Would you
8 thanks so much
9 coming
10 trip

page 13

Greetings and introductions
Good morning. You must be … I'm …
Welcome to IGS.
It's nice to finally meet you face to face.
I'd like to introduce you to Anke Schmidt.
Anke, this is Peter Manser …
Nice to meet you(, too).

Small talk questions
How was your flight?
And is this your first time in Hamburg?

Offering hospitality
May I take your coat?
If you'd like to take a seat …
Would you care for coffee or tea?

Saying goodbye
Thanks so much for a good meeting.
Thanks for coming.
We'll be in contact by email …
Bye.
Have a nice trip!
So long for now.

4 1 introduce
2 finally
3 May
4 kind
5 like
6 care
7 get
8 contact
9 pleasure; journey
10 long

page 14

5 1 – c – E
2 – e – A
3 – a – F
4 – f – B
5 – b – D
6 – d – C

page 15

7 1 *Do*
2 *Do*
3 *Don't*; Do
4 Do; Don't
5 Don't
6 Don't; Do; don't
7 Do
8 Do

8 1 b
2 a
3 a
4 b
5 a
6 b

page 16

10 1 F
2 ?
3 F
4 F
5 T
6 F

(Suggested answer)
Notes
interested customer
write him an email next week to thank him for
stopping by the stand

follow-up to offer help again and to send out a new
catalogue

11 1 introduce; ask
2 enjoying
3 anything
4 free; glad
5 brochure
6 put
7 mind; email

page 17

12 1 May/Could I ask/have your name?
2 Are you looking for anything special/in particular?
3 Please feel free to ask me any questions.
4 Can I interest you in a brochure?/Would you like/care for a brochure?
5 Would you like to put your name on the mailing list?/Would you like to be on our mailing list?
6 Do you mind if I take/Would you mind if I took your business card?
7 I'll email/phone you next week to see if I can help you with any of our products.

13 1 b
2 f
3 g
4 d
5 a
6 c
7 e

page 18

15 1 d
2 b
3 a
4 e
5 c

page 19

16 a 2
b 9
c 4
d 1
e 6
f 7
g 3
h 5
i 8

UNIT 3

page 21

1 (model answers)

What went wrong
too much noise
poor listening
unhelpful
didn't connect the customer
shouting so that the customer can hear it

What went right
polite and friendly
helpful
patient
good listening
asked to repeat information
connected the customer to the right extension

1 May I help you?
2 you repeat that, please?
3 I'm afraid
4 Would you like me
5 Thanks for your call.

page 22

2
1	May I help you?	6	I'm afraid
2	just a moment	7	terribly sorry
3	would you like	8	Yes, certainly
4	Thanks for holding.	9	I'll make sure
5	catch	10	no problem

Message
Message for: Eva Lang
Caller: John Richards
Company: Customer Zone Software
Message: Call him as soon as possible today
on 0044 7721 332558.

page 23

3
1	c	5	g
2	e	6	b
3	d	7	h
4	a	8	f

page 24

4
1	put; through	4	cut off
2	look up	5	got through to
3	speak up	6	get back to

5
1	hold	6	back to
2	put	7	afraid
3	speak	8	repeat
4	May	9	I'll make sure
5	leave	10	anything

page 25

7
1	Thomas	4	503
2	software	5	549822
3	1	6	price list

page 26

1	a	4	a
2	b	5	a
3	b		

8 Yes, Peter Busch followed all the steps.

a	2	h	5
b	6	i	1
c	9	j	7
d	8	k	10
e	4	l	3
f	1	m	4
g	7		

page 27

9
1	g	5	e
2	f	6	c
3	b	7	a
4	d	8	h

10
1	h	7	i
2	d	8	b
3	k	9	j
4	a	10	e
5	l	11	g
6	f	12	c

page 28

11
1	c	4	a
2	d	5	b
3	e		

13
1 confirm
2 holding
3 set up
4 appreciate
5 catch
6 convenient
7 once
8 would you
9 extension

The hidden word is: courteous

UNIT 4

page 30

First approach
1 24%
2 11%
3 16%
4 7%
5 62%

1 Caller 1 has called for help and caller 2 is placing an order.

Call 1
Customer: Mr Anderson from a bank
Customer interested in: help with bank's IT system
Follow-up: will call back in half an hour and maybe send out a technician

Call 2
Customer: Jochen Wagner, a regular customer
Customer interested in: placing an order
Follow-up: will send out order straight away

page 31

2 Call 1
1 It seems
2 Let me just
3 I understand; Is that right?
4 'll check; 'll call you
5 all right
6 Could I assist

Call 2
7 let me just pull up
8 do for
9 'll flag; straight away
10 Thank you

3
1	c	5	a
2	f	6	g
3	d	7	b
4	h	8	e

page 32

4 1 May I help you?
2 Could you give me your customer number, please?

3 I'd just like to confirm your contact details.
4 OK, let me just repeat that.
5 Is that right?
6 could I go over your order again?
7 Could I help you with anything else?

page 33

5
1 place
2 payment
3 dispatched
4 rush
5 give; catalogue
6 quote
7 invoice
8 overnight

6 (Model answers)

1 I'm afraid I didn't quite catch that. Could you speak up a bit, please?
2 How can/may I help you today?/ assist you today?
3 I'm sorry I didn't quite understand/catch that.
4 How many packages would you like/are you interested in?
5 Would you mind giving me your address?/Could I/May I have your address?
6 Let me just read that back to you/repeat that. ... Could I help/assist you with anything else?
7 You should receive/get it by Tuesday (be specific!). If you haven't got it by then, please give me a call. Thanks for your business. Bye for now.

page 34

7
1 b   4 b
2 a   5 a
3 b

The following sentences are in the conversation:
1 – 3 – 4 – 7 – 9 – 10 – 12

8
1 We just need to clarify a few things.
2 Is everything clear so far?
3 Could you explain what you've done so far?
4 That means you need to install some software.
5 What does OS stand for?
6 This is what I'm going to do.
7 Let me just talk you through the steps.

page 35

9 (Phrases in brackets also possible.)
1 Really? (Is that so?)
2 You don't say! (Really?)
3 Right. (I see.)
4 Of course. (Uh uh)

page 36

10
1 b
2 b
3 a
4 b
5 c
6 a

11 Across
1 clarification
5 satisfaction
6 explanation
8 delivery

a assistance
b explanation
c offer; payment

Down
2 assistance
3 payment
4 offer
7 order

UNIT 5

page 38

First Approach
(suggested answers)

1 F   6 T
2 F   7 T
3 T   8 F
4 F   9 F
5 F

1
1 b   4 e
2 d   5 c
3 a

email: a, b, c, e
letter: d
You can tell because of the salutations and closes.

page 40

2 (suggested answers)

1 *Hi Hugo ... All the best*
2 Dear Walter ... Best wishes
3 Dear Janet and Mario ... Best wishes/Kind regards
4 Dear Ms Elan ... Yours sincerely or AE: Sincerely (yours)
5 Dear Mr and Mrs Duchard... (Kind) regards/Best wishes
6 Dear Sir or Madam ... Yours faithfully or AE: Sincerely (yours)

3
1 He probably doesn't know him very well.
2 At the Business Executive Conference.
3 A catalogue including prices.
4 Mr Vogel will phone Mr Davis on Thursday to arrange a meeting.

a It was a pleasure ...
b I am enclosing our latest catalogue ...
c I will phone you on Thursday ...
d If you have any further questions, please do not hesitate to contact me.
e As requested ...
f I look forward to welcoming you as a new and valued customer.

page 41

4
1 b   5 e
2 f   6 g
3 d   7 c
4 a

1 It was a pleasure to speak to you (5e)
2 We are delighted to have you as a new customer (2f)

3 If you are satisfied with the results (6g)
4 I will pay you a visit personally (7c)
5 If you have any further questions (3d)
6 I look forward to seeing you next week (1b)
7 Thank you for choosing our company (4a)

page 42

5 Dear Mr Vogt
b – f – a – d

Dear Manfred
e – c – h – g

page 43

6 1 In regard to your phone call …
2 Thanks for your phone call this morning.
3 I am writing to let you know …
4 Just a quick email to let you know …
5 I am delighted to inform you …
6 I'm glad to tell you …
7 I would appreciate it if we could …
8 It'd be great if we could …
9 If you have any other questions, please don't hesitate to contact me.
10 I look forward to seeing you next week.
11 Let me know if you need any other help.
12 Looking forward to seeing you next week.

7 1 regard   5 hearing
2 pleased   6 would; convenience
3 of   7 reply
4 back   8 just

page 44

8 This email goes against the five Cs. It is unclear, incomplete, has too much unnecessary information, the language is not courteous enough and there are a lot of mistakes (spelling, punctuation, paragraphs in wrong order, salutation).

(model answer)

Dear Ms Jones

It was a pleasure to meet you recently at the Global Concepts Trade Fair. I hope you enjoyed the fair as much as I did.

As you requested, I've attached our latest price list. I would also like to send you our latest catalogue. Could you please confirm your postal address?

I would welcome the chance to find out more about your customer needs. I would like to phone you at the end of the week to arrange a meeting. Would Friday at 14.00 be convenient for you?

Thanks for your interest in Select Systems GmbH. I look forward to speaking to you soon.

Yours sincerely

9 1 c
2 a
3 b

email: a, b, (documents are 'attached')
letter: c (magazine is 'enclosed')

UNIT 6

page 48

2 do: 1, 4, 7, 8
don't: 2, 3, 5, 6

3 1 b (bank)
2 a (airport)
3 c (department store)

	complaint	response
Dialogue 1	poor service at bank	apologizes for service and staff; invites customer into the office to talk without interruption
Dialogue 2	flight has been cancelled	empathizes, explains reason and offers help
Dialogue 3	customer has been over-charged	offers to refund money and then agrees to exchange jumper

page 49

4 1 sorry; hear
2 seems; problem
3 let me apologize
4 understand
5 inconvenienced
6 let me see; assist
7 appears; mistake
8 refund
9 problem; be glad

5 (Suggested answers)
1 *There seems to be a misunderstanding.*
2 I'm afraid there's a problem/mix-up with your order.
3 It appears that some of the parts weren't included in the shipment.
4 It seems that your email didn't get through.
5 I'm afraid there's been a delay with your order. Your order should arrive by (early next week).
6 It appears that a mistake has been made.

page 50

6 1 b   4 c
2 e   5 a
3 d

7 1 Excuse me
2 seems to be
3 I'd like to say
4 I can see how
5 understand
6 Would you mind
7 straight away
8 make sure
9 inconvenienced
10 I'd be glad

page 51

8

What the receptionist did:	What the receptionist said:
1 *listened*	–
2 apologized	First of all, I'd like to say how sorry I am.
3 repeated	So, if I understand you correctly, …
4 asked for	Would you mind giving me more details … ?
5 took	I'll speak to housekeeping straight away.
6 offered	Since you've been so inconvenienced by this incident, I'd be glad to offer you …

page 52

9
1 d   6 f
2 a   7 e
3 g   8 c
4 i   9 b
5 h

page 53

11 1 We are very concerned to hear
2 We very much regret
3 We assure you that we are doing everything we can
4 The problem has now been resolved
5 Once again, we apologize

a We are very concerned to hear that your order from last month has not reached you.
b We very much regret …; Once again, we apologize for the inconvenience.
c We very much regret the frustration this has caused you.
d The delay was due to …
e … your order has been sent to you by overnight post.

page 54

12 1 c   4 e
2 d   5 b
3 a

13 (Model answer)
These problems would be best handled by a phone call (to schedule a meeting) and then a personal visit. The problem-solving steps shoud be followed in a face-to-face meeting. Email should be used to follow-up the action points of the meeting.

pages 56–57

Test yourself!

Across
3 appears
4 attentive
6 catch
8 responsible
9 ring
16 anything else
19 assist
20 delighted
21 afraid
22 make sure
24 confirm
25 go over
26 forward
27 hesitate

Down
1 appreciate
2 rapport
5 empathy
6 convenient
7 browsing
10 straight away
11 clarify
12 satisfaction
13 welcome
14 apologize
15 introduce
17 small talk
18 mind
23 regards

Transcripts

UNIT 2, EXERCISE 2

1
A Good morning, Ms Richards. How are you today?
B Fine, thanks. Ah, is Frau Schultz free at the moment? I have a quick question about my account.
A Yes, she's at the desk over there. Just go on over …

2
A Hello. May I help you with something?
B No, thank you. I'm just looking.
A Well, if you need help, just let me know.

3
A Hello, My name is Jaime Rodriguez. I have a reservation.
B One moment, please. Let me check. Ah yes. Could you just fill in this form, please, Mr Rodriguez?

4
A Hello. May I help you?
B Yes, I have an appointment with Ms Jilek. My name is John Roberts.
A Roberts? Ah, yes. Please take a seat over there, Mr Roberts. I'll tell her you're here.

5
A Hello. May I help you?
B Yes, I'm with IBT Corporation. My name is Roger Alle. I have a few questions about your products.
A Ah, nice to meet you, Mr Alle. I'm Sarah Levinson. So, how can I help you?

UNIT 2, EXERCISE 3

Fritz Good morning, you must be Peter Manser. I'm Fritz Heinle. Welcome to IGS.
Peter Thank you. It's nice to finally meet you face to face.
Fritz Yes, we've talked so much on the phone, I feel like I know you already. Peter, I'd like to introduce you to Anke Schmidt, our customer services manager. Anke, this is Peter Manser from TopForm in Bristol.
Peter Nice to meet you, Ms Schmidt.
Anke Nice to meet you, too.
Fritz So, if you'd just come this way …
Anke How was your flight from Bristol?
Peter It was fine. It even arrived a bit early.
Anke And is this your first time in Hamburg?
Peter No, it's my third. I've been here a couple times as a tourist. I really like the city.
Fritz So, here we are. May I take your coat?
Peter Oh, that's very kind of you.
Fritz If you'd like to take a seat …
Peter Thank you.
Fritz Would you care for coffee or tea?
Peter Tea would be nice, with two sugars.
        * * *
Peter So, here's my taxi. Well, thanks so much for a good meeting. It was great to meet both of you.
Fritz The same for us. Thanks for coming. It was a very productive meeting. So, we'll be in contact by email as usual.

Peter Yes, of course. Bye.
Anke Have a nice trip! Bye
Fritz So long for now.

UNIT 2, EXERCISE 10

Otto May I introduce myself? I'm Otto Brandt. I work for Metro GmbH. May I ask your name?
Lewis Lewis Gillan – I'm with Accutech UK. Nice to meet you.
Otto Pleased to meet you, too. So, Mr Gillan, how are you enjoying the trade fair?
Lewis It's my first time here, actually. It's very interesting. Lots of good contacts. What about you?
Otto Oh, I'm enjoying it too. We're here every year and it's quite an important event for us. Well, then, are you looking for anything in particular?
Lewis Right now I'm just browsing.
Otto OK, but please feel free to ask me any questions. I'd be glad to go over our products and try to find something suitable for your company.
Lewis Thanks, that's very helpful. (a few minutes later) Well, thank you.
Otto Ah, can I interest you in a brochure? It has information about our company and our full range of products.
Lewis Yes, thank you.
Otto Here you are. And we've got a new catalogue coming out next week. We're launching some exciting new products. Would you like to put your name on our mailing list?
Lewis Yes, that would be good.
Otto Do you mind if I take your business card? I'll make sure you're on our list. And here's my card. I'll send you a quick email next week to see if I can help you with any of our products.
Lewis That sounds fine. It was nice to meet you.
Otto The same here. Enjoy the rest of the fair.

UNIT 3, EXERCISE 1

Call 1
A Yeah?
B Hello. This is Marjorie Heighton. I'd like to confirm my appointment with Peter Gore.
A Um … sorry … what did you say?
B I'd like to confirm my appointment with Peter Gore, please.
A Well, this is the wrong number for that. Uh, wait. (puts phone on hold) Hello? Mrs … um … Hate …
B Heighton. Marjorie Heighton.
A Look, I'm not responsible for that. You'll have to call Peter's secretary.
B OK. Can you give me the phone number or connect me?
A Yeah, OK. Does anybody know Peter's extension?

Call 2
A Hello, Martha Greer speaking. May I help you?
B Hello. This is Donald Kraft. Could I speak to Anthony Smithson, please?

A Sorry, could you repeat that, please?

B Yes, this is Donald Kraft. I'd like to speak to Anthony Smithson.

A I'm afraid you've got the wrong extension, Mr Kraft. You need to speak to Mr Smithson's office. Would you like me to connect you?

B Yes, that would be great.

A OK, Mr Kraft. I'm putting you through now. Thanks for your call.

UNIT 3, EXERCISE 2

Call 1

12

Elke Good morning. Apex Industries. May I help you?

John Yes, this is John Richards from Customer Zone Software. I'd like to speak to Eva Lang, please. Could you put me through to her?

Elke Of course, just a moment, please. ... Oh, it seems that her line is engaged. Could you hold a moment? Or would you like to leave a message?

John I'd prefer to hold for just a minute or two.

...

Elke Mr Richards. Thanks for holding. I'm putting you through to Ms Lang's office now. If you get cut off for some reason, please get back to me.

John I'm sorry. Could you speak up a bit? I didn't quite catch that.

Elke Sure. I'm connecting you now to the Ms Lang's office. If you don't get through, please ring again. We're having some problems with our phone system.

Call 2

13

Elke Good morning. Apex Industries.

John This is John Richards again. I'm afraid I got cut off when you tried to put me through.

Elke I'm terribly sorry about that.

John I really need to get through to Ms Lang this afternoon. Could I leave a message for her to ring me back as soon as possible?

Elke Yes certainly Mr Richards. Could I have your phone number, please?

John Yes, I'm calling from my mobile. It's 0044 7721 332558.

Elke Right. So, that's 0044 7721 332558. I'll make sure she calls you back today. Could I help you with anything else?

John Would it be possible to have her mobile number? Could you perhaps look it up for me?

Elke Yes, that's no problem. I've got it right here. It's 49 for Germany, then 156 8877944.

John Let me just repeat that. That's 49 156 8877944. Thanks once again. Bye for now.

Elke You're welcome. Goodbye.

UNIT 3, EXERCISE 5

Uta Edelweiss Beverages, Uta Maly.

Henry Hello. Could I have extension 226, please?

Uta I'm sorry, the line's engaged. Could you please hold? ... Sir, the line's free now. I'll put you through.

Henry Thanks.

Emil Service department.

Henry I'd like to speak to Mr Schmidt, please. Is he available at the moment?

Emil May I ask who's calling?

Henry Henry Jones. I'm calling from ABC Ltd in London.

Emil Just a moment please, Mr Jones. I'll see if he's available. ... Mr Jones? I'm afraid Herr Schmidt's in a meeting. Would you like to leave a message?

Henry Yes, please ask him to get back to me as soon as possible. My number's 44 207 563 361.

Emil I'm afraid I didn't catch that. Could you repeat the number, please?

Henry Yes, it's 44 for the UK, then 207 563 361.

Emil OK, I'll make sure he gets the message. Is there anything else I can do for you?

Henry No, thanks.

Emil Goodbye, then, Mr Jones. Thanks for calling.

Henry You're welcome. Goodbye.

UNIT 3, EXERCISE 7

Thomas Hello.

15

Busch Hello, this is Peter Busch from Tannen GmbH. Is that Mr Thomas?

Thomas Yes, it is.

Busch Hello, Mr Thomas. I got your contact details from one of my colleagues. I'm calling to see if I could possibly interest you in our new line of customer tracking software.

Thomas Oh yes. What good timing. You know, we've been thinking about updating the way we keep customer information here and I've started making some enquiries about new software.

Busch Really? I'm glad I've phoned you then. I'm in the area next week. Perhaps I could stop by your office and show you the latest software.

Thomas That sounds good. Could we set up a meeting on Wednesday, say, at 1?

Busch OK, that suits me fine. Let me just make sure I have the right address. That's 500 Azan Road, correct?

Thomas That's the main building. I'm actually across the street, at 503. Let me give you my mobile number, just in case. It's 07887 549822.

Busch 887 ... I'm sorry, I didn't catch the last bit.

Thomas 549822.

Busch 549822. OK, Mr Thomas, let me just confirm that. That's Wednesday at 1 pm and you're at 503 Azan Road. Mobile number 07887 549822.

Thomas That's right. In the meantime, could you give me an idea of a price range for the tracking software?

Busch Sure. I'll email you a complete price list straight away and I'll also send you a PDF version of our brochure, if that's ok.

Thomas Yes, that would be very helpful. Thank you very much.

Busch Is there anything else I can do for you before our meeting on Wednesday?

Thomas No, I think that's it.

Busch OK. I look forward to seeing you on Wednesday, Mr Thomas.

Thomas Yes, see you then. Goodbye.

Busch Goodbye.

UNIT 3, EXERCISE 10

Nathalie Âllo.

16

Susanne Hello, may I speak to Nathalie Laurent, please?

Nathalie Speaking.

Susanne	Nathalie, this is Susanne Finster from Brand AG. We met at the trade fair last week.
Nathalie	Ah, yes. Right. How are you?
Susanne	Fine, thanks. Nathalie, I'm calling to see if we could set up a meeting. You wanted me to do a presentation on our services and I'll be in Metz next week.
Nathalie	Next week? Let just check my diary. What day exactly?
Susanne	Would Tuesday be convenient for you, at 9 am?
Nathalie	Tuesday looks good, but I'm busy at 9. How about 11 o'clock instead?
Susanne	Sounds good. OK, Nathalie, that's Tuesday at 11 o'clock. I look forward to seeing you.
Nathalie	Same here. Thanks for calling. Bye.
Susanne	Bye.

UNIT 4, EXERCISE 1

🎧 Call 1

17

Customer	Hello.
Agent	Hello, is that Mr Anderson?
Customer	Yes, speaking.
Agent	This is Klaus Heinrich from NewTech Call Centre. I'm ringing because I got a message that you called our QuickHelp line. It seems that you need some assistance.
Customer	Oh, great. Yes, there's a bit of a problem with our bank's IT system. When we try to view our customer accounts, the program crashes …
Agent	Mr Anderson, let me just type this in … one moment … OK. Could you tell me when exactly it crashes?
Customer	Well, it's hard to tell what causes it. The normal screen comes up and asks you to type in the name first, then hit return, then type in the password. It seems OK at first, the new page comes up, then there's a funny clicking noise like the computer's trying to do something. This goes on quite a long time, then the screen just freezes.
Agent	OK, so, as I understand it, the problem begins with entering the password. Is that right?
Customer	Yes, that's right.
Agent	And how long have you had this problem?
Customer	Well, I've only tried it twice but then thought I'd better call you. So, when can you take care of this? Our work depends on the system being up and running all the time.
Agent	Yes, I can understand how important it is. I think we can send someone out to you this afternoon. I'll check the service technicians' schedule and I'll call you back in half an hour. Does that sound all right?
Customer	That sounds good.
Agent	Could I assist you with anything else today?
Customer	No, but thanks for asking. I'll be waiting for you to ring back.

🎧 Call 2

18

Agent	Good afternoon, Media Concepts. Gerry speaking. How can I help you?
Customer	Hello, I'd like to place an order, please. The name's Jochen Wagner. I'm already a regular customer.

Agent	Could I have your account number, please?
Customer	Mmm, yes, it's 55878.
Agent	55878 … One moment, let me just pull up your customer file on my screen. Right. So, Mr Wagner, what can I do for you?
Customer	I'd like to place an order for some spare parts and was wondering if it would be possible to receive them by Thursday? It's quite urgent.
Agent	Well, if the items are in stock, it should be no problem to send them out straight away. What exactly would you like to order? Could you give me the first order number, please?
Customer	OK, that's EJT53021. I'd like two of them. And the other order number is … EJS36899. I need eight.
Agent	Was that EJS for Sam?
Customer	Right.
Agent	OK, let me repeat that. EJT for Thomas 53021, two items. And EJS for Sam 36899, eight items. Is that correct?
Customer	That's right. Are they in stock?
Agent	Yes, they are. I'll flag your order as urgent so that the items will be sent out straight away. You should receive the order in a couple of days, and definitely by Thursday.
Customer	Sounds good.
Agent	Can I help you with anything else today?
Customer	No, that's all for today, thank you.
Agent	OK, Mr Wagner, thank you for your order. Goodbye.

UNIT 4, EXERCISE 7

🎧
20

Operative	Hello. Susanne speaking. How can I help you?
Customer	Hello. I hope I'm at the right place. I just got a new MP3 player – the i-go – and I can't seem to get it to work. I'm trying to install the software and it just won't work.
Operative	OK, first of all, is that the i-go mini or the i-go maxi?
Customer	The mini.
Operative	Right. So what exactly is the problem? Could you explain what you've done so far?
Customer	Well, I put in the CD to install the software and it seemed to work. *(Right.)* But now I can't open the window. *(OK.)* There's some message about something to do with the system and a number.
Operative	I see. It could be a systems requirement problem.
Customer	Sorry, what does that mean?
Operative	Well, the systems requirement for the i-go is OS 10 version 10.1.4. That means you need to have that version or a more recent one on your computer or you can't run the software for the i-go.
Customer	I see.
Operative	So, could you tell me which operating system you have on your computer?
Customer	No, sorry. I'm afraid I'm not very good with computers, as you can tell. I got this i-go for Christmas and I didn't think it would be so difficult to use.
Operative	Oh, don't worry. We just need to clarify a few things, then you'll have no trouble.

OK, do you see the green box on the upper left-hand corner of your screen? *(Uh huh.)* When you click on it you'll see a menu. The first item on the menu says 'about your computer'. Are you following me all right?

Customer	Yes.
Operative	OK, click on that and you'll see what operating system you have. Are you having any trouble seeing that? The letters OS followed by some numbers?
Customer	Ah … yes, uhm … it's OS 10.1. Is that what you mean?
Operative	That's right and we've found your problem. You need to upgrade your system before you can install the software for your i-go.
Customer	And how do I do that?
Operative	Oh, that's very easy. Let me just talk you through the steps …

* * *

Operative	So, that will take a while to download, but once it does, you can just use it to upgrade your system free of charge. Then you'll have no trouble installing the i-go software.
Customer	Great. Thanks so much.
Operative	You're welcome. By the way, have you registered with us?
Customer	No, I don't think so. Could you tell me more about that?
Operative	Well, if you register with us, we can activate your guarantee and you'll have two years of free service …

UNIT 4, EXERCISE 9

21

C I left a message for the call centre manager to call me back. That was three days ago and I've heard nothing from him.

A Really? I'm so sorry. Let me see if I can help you …

C I've emailed your helpline three times, but the emails have all been returned.

A You don't say! I'm sorry about that. We must have had a problem with our server. It seems to be working all right now though. How I can help you?

C I'm having trouble with my television. It turns on and I can see the picture, but I can't seem to get any sound.

A Right. OK, I'm going to need to ask you some questions …

C Your product is very good, but I'd like more information on an upgraded model.

A Of course. I think I can suggest something for you …

UNIT 5, EXERCISE 9

Message 1
22
Hello, my name is Carmen Lopez, that's L–O–P–E–Z. I'm going to be in Hamburg next week and I'd like to make a reservation for a single room with a bath for two nights, um that's Tuesday and Wednesday night, I think the dates are 5 to 7 May. Could you just confirm the reservation in writing? You have my contact details in your file. Oh, and could you also send me a list of events like concerts and plays for those evenings? Thanks.

Message 2
23
Hello, I'm calling about your catering service. We're having an office party in two weeks' time for about 50 people and I wanted to see some menus and get your price list. Could you send something asap? You can contact me at Hsu – that's H–S–U – @htk-systems.de. I'll repeat that. That's Hsu@htk-systems.de. Thanks.

Message 3
24
Hello, this is Markus Steffan calling again. I need the specifications for the 830T laser printer. Do you think you could email them to me this afternoon? Thanks and talk soon.

UNIT 6, EXERCISE 3

Dialogue 1
25

Customer	Excuse me. I'd like to make a complaint.
Bank manager	Oh, I'm sorry to hear that. What seems to be the problem?
Customer	Your bank service is just awful. I was here last week to take care of some banking transactions. The line was very long since there was only one teller. I asked a bank employee to bring in another teller, but he said they were too busy with more important work. So it took me over an hour to get my business done. I'm going to change to the Clyde Bank!
Bank manager	First of all, let me apologize for the poor service and unhelpful member of staff. It seems that you went through a terrible time getting your business done. Why don't you come into my office where we can talk without any interruptions … ?

Dialogue 2
26

Customer	You really must help me! My flight to Manchester has been cancelled. This is a huge problem for me since I must get there by tomorrow at 10.00 for an important meeting. If I don't get there in time, I could lose a very special client! I'm a frequent flier with your airline, so I expect you to do something about this straight away.
Airline agent	I understand the stress you must be feeling. I'm afraid we've had to make a lot of cancellations lately and I'm sorry that you've been so inconvenienced. So, let me see how I can assist you …

Dialogue 3
27

Customer	Excuse me. I bought this jumper at your shop yesterday. When I got home, I looked at the receipt and saw that you had overcharged me ten euros.
Floor manager	Oh, I'm so sorry. It appears that our shop assistant made a mistake. I'll be happy to refund your money.
Customer	Actually, I've also decided that the jumper is not really the right colour, so I'd like to exchange them for something in red or yellow.
Floor manager	That's no problem. I'll be glad to help you

A–Z word list

A

abbreviation [əˌbriːviˈeɪʃn] — Abkürzung
ability [əˈbɪləti] — Fähigkeit, Können
to accept [əkˈsept] — akzeptieren, annehmen
acceptable [əkˈseptəbl] — annehmbar, passend
according to [əˈkɔːdɪŋ tə] — entsprechend, nach
accountancy [əˈkaʊntənsi] — Buchhaltung, Buchführung
accurate [ˈækjərət] — genau, richtig
to acknowledge [əkˈnɒlɪdʒ] — (an)erkennen, zustimmen
to activate [ˈæktɪveɪt] — aktivieren
to adjust [əˈdʒʌst] — einstellen, justieren
advantage, to take ~ of [ˌteɪk ədˈvɑːntɪdʒ əv] — sich zu Nutze machen, ausnützen
advert(isement) [ˈædvɜːt, ədˈvɜːtɪsmənt] — Anzeige
to affect [əˈfekt] — sich auswirken auf, beeinflussen
after-sales service [ˈɑːftəseɪlz sɜːvɪs] — Kundendienst
agent, call center [ˈeɪdʒənt] — Angestellte/r im Call-Center
aggressive [əˈɡresɪv] — aggressiv
aim [eɪm] — Ziel
to align [əˈlaɪn] — ausrichten
alternative [ɔːlˈtɜːnətɪv] — Alternative
anger [ˈæŋɡə] — Ärger, Verärgerung
to annoy [əˈnɔɪ] — ärgern
to apologize [əˈpɒlədʒaɪz] — sich entschuldigen
appointment [əˈpɔɪntmənt] — Termin, Verabredung
to appreciate [əˈpriːʃieɪt] — zu schätzen wissen, dankbar sein (für)
approach, first ~ [fɜːst əˈprəʊtʃ] — erster Kontakt
appropriate [əˈprəʊpriət] — geeignet, angemessen
approximately [əˈprɒksɪmətli] — ungefähr, zirka
to arrange [əˈreɪndʒ] — arrangieren, organisieren
to assist [əˈsɪst] — helfen, unterstützen
assistance [əˈsɪstəns] — Hilfe, Unterstützung
assurance, life ~ [ˈlaɪf əʃʊərəns] — Lebensversicherung
to assure [əˈʃʊə] — zusichern, versprechen
to attach [əˈtætʃ] — beilegen, -fügen
attempt [əˈtempt] — Versuch
to attend [əˈtend] — teilnehmen
attention [əˈtenʃn] — Aufmerksamkeit
attention, to pay ~ to [peɪ əˈtenʃn tə] — achten auf, beachten
attentive [əˈtentɪv] — aufmerksam
audience [ˈɔːdiəns] — Publikum
automated [ˈɔːtəmeɪtɪd] — automatisiert
available, to be ~ [əˈveɪləbl] — (am Telefon) zu sprechen sein
average [ˈævərɪdʒ] — durchschnittlich
to avoid [əˈvɔɪd] — vermeiden
awareness [əˈweənəs] — Bewusstsein

B

background [ˈbækɡraʊnd] — Hintergrund
base, customer ~ [ˈkʌstəmə beɪs] — Kundenstamm, -bestand
bellhop (AE) [ˈbelhɒp] — Page, Hoteljunge
benefit [ˈbenɪfɪt] — Vorteil, zusätzliche Leistung, Vergünstigung
bind, to be in a ~ [bi ɪn ə ˈbaɪnd] — in der Klemme sein
to block [blɒk] — sperren, stoppen
to boast of sth [ˈbəʊst əv] — stolz auf etw sein
body language [ˈbɒdi læŋɡwɪdʒ] — Körpersprache
bond [bɒnd] — Band, (Ver-)Bindung
to browse [braʊz] — stöbern, surfen
business area [ˌbɪznəs ˈeəriə] — Geschäftsbereich

C

call, to receive a ~ [rɪˈsiːv ə kɔːl] — einen Anruf erhalten
cancellation [ˌkænsəˈleɪʃn] — Stornierung, Absage
to capture [ˈkæptʃə] — gewinnen
to care for [ˈkeə fə] — möchten, mögen
care, to take ~ of [teɪk ˈkeər əv] — sich kümmern um, erledigen
carry [ˌkæri] — führen
to carry out [ˌkæri ˈaʊt] — durchführen
case, just in ~ [dʒʌst ɪn ˈkeɪs] — nur für den (Not-)Fall
cashier [kæˈʃɪə] — Kassierer/in
to catch [kætʃ] — verstehen
catering [ˈkeɪtərɪŋ] — Gastronomie
to chew [tʃuː] — kauen
clarification [ˌklærɪfɪˈkeɪʃn] — Erläuterung(en), Klarstellung
to clarify [ˈklærəfaɪ] — (auf)klären, klarstellen
clerk [klɑːk] — (Büro-)Angestellte/r
clue [kluː] — Hinweis, Tipp
to combine [kəmˈbaɪn] — verbinden, kombinieren
communication skills [kəˌmjuːnɪˈkeɪʃən skɪlz] — kommunikative Fertigkeiten
to compare [kəmˈpeə] — vergleichen
compensation [ˌkɒmpənˈseɪʃn] — Schaden(s)ersatz, Entschädigung
competition [ˌkɒmpəˈtɪʃn] — Konkurrenz
competitor [kəmˈpetɪtə] — Konkurrent/in, Mitbewerber/in
complaint [kəmˈpleɪnt] — Beanstandung, Reklamation
compliment [ˈkɒmplɪmənt] — Kompliment
concept [ˈkɒnsept] — Konzept, Idee
concerned, to be ~ [bi kənˈsɜːnd] — besorgt sein
concise [kənˈsaɪs] — präzise, knapp
to confirm [kənˈfɜːm] — bestätigen
to connect [kəˈnekt] — verbinden
consignment [kənˈsaɪnmənt] — Sendung, Lieferung
contract [ˈkɒntrækt] — Vertrag
convenience [kənˈviːniəns] — Komfort, Bequemlichkeit
convenient [kənˈviːniənt] — bequem, angenehm, passend
convention [kənˈvenʃn] — Brauch, Konvention
correspondence [ˌkɒrɪˈspɒndəns] — Korrespondenz
courteous [ˈkɜːtiəs] — höflich
courtesy [ˈkɜːtəsi] — Höflichkeit
to crash [kræʃ] — abstürzen
to create [kriˈeɪt] — (er)schaffen
to cross-sell [ˌkrɒs ˈsel] — zusätzlich verkaufen
crucial [ˈkruːʃl] — entscheidend
current [ˈkʌrənt] — aktuell
customer-centred [ˈkʌstəmə sentəd] — kundenorientiert
customer-friendly [ˈkʌstəmə frendli] — verbraucher-, kundenfreundlich
cut off, to get ~ [get ˌkʌt ˈɒf] — unterbrochen werden

D

database [ˈdeɪtəbeɪs] — Datenbank
to deal with sb/sth [ˈdiːl wɪð] — mit jdm zutun haben; sich um etw kümmern
decision [dɪˈsɪʒn] — Entscheidung
definitely [ˈdefɪnətli] — bestimmt, sicher(lich)
to defuse [ˌdiːˈfjuːz] — entschärfen
to delay [dɪˈleɪ] — aufschieben, hinauszögern
delay [dɪˈleɪ] — Verzögerung
delighted [dɪˈlaɪtɪd] — (sehr) erfreut, entzückt
to deliver [dɪˈlɪvə] — abliefern, überbringen
delivery [dɪˈlɪvəri] — Zustellung, (Aus-)Lieferung
demand [dɪˈmɑːnd] — Nachfrage, Bedarf

demanding [dɪˈmɑːndɪŋ]	anstrengend, anspruchsvoll
to **demonstrate** [ˈdemənstreɪt]	demonstrieren, zeigen
department [dɪˈpɑːtmənt]	Abteilung
department store	Kauf-, Warenhaus
[dɪˈpɑːtmənt stɔː]	
dependable [dɪˈpendəbl]	zuverlässig, verlässlich
desk [desk]	Arbeitsplatz, Schalter
development [dɪˈveləpmənt]	Entwicklung
diplomacy [dɪˈpləʊməsi]	Diplomatie
directory [dəˈrektəri]	Telefonbuch
disconnected, to get ~	unterbrochen werden
[get ˌdɪskəˈnektɪd]	(am Telefon)
discount [ˈdɪskaʊnt]	Rabatt, Skonto
dismay, to my ~ [tə maɪ dɪsˈmeɪ]	zu meiner Verärgerung
to **dispatch** [dɪˈspætʃ]	(ab)senden, (aus)liefern
dissatisfied, to be ~	unzufrieden sein
[bi dɪsˈsætɪsfaɪd]	
to **distract** [dɪˈstrækt]	ablenken
distraction [dɪˈstrækʃn]	Ablenkung
due [djuː]	fällig, Fälligkeits-
duty [ˈdjuːti]	Aufgabe
duty, to go beyond the call of ~	mehr als seine Pflicht tun
[gəʊ bɪˌjɒnd ðə kɔːl əv ˈdjuːti]	

E

edge [edʒ]	Vorteil, Vorsprung
effective [ɪˈfektɪv]	wirksam, wirkungsvoll
efficient [ɪˈfɪʃnt]	effizient
empathy [ˈempəθi]	Einfühlung(svermögen), Mitgefühl
to **enclose** [ɪnˈkləʊz]	beilegen, beifügen
encounter [ɪnˈkaʊntə]	Begegnung
engaged, the line is ~	die Leitung ist besetzt
[ðə laɪn ɪz ɪnˈgeɪdʒd]	
engagement [ɪnˈgeɪdʒmənt]	Verabredung
enquiry [ɪnˈkwaɪəri]	Anfrage
to **ensure** [ɪnˈʃʊə]	dafür sorgen, dass; gewährleisten
equipment [ɪˈkwɪpmənt]	Ausrüstung
equivalent [ɪˈkwɪvələnt]	Entsprechung
especially [ɪˈspeʃəli]	besonders
essential [ɪˈsenʃl]	wesentlich
to **establish** [ɪˈstæblɪʃ]	herstellen, bilden
estimate [ˈestɪmət]	Kostenvoranschlag
event [ɪˈvent]	Ereignis, Veranstaltung
excerpt [ˈeksɜːpt]	Auszug
to **exchange** [ɪksˈtʃeɪndʒ]	austauschen
exchange [ɪksˈtʃeɪndʒ]	Umtausch
to **exhale** [eksˈheɪl]	ausatmen
exhibit area [ɪgˌzɪbɪt ˈeəriə]	Ausstellungsfläche
to **expect** [ɪkˈspekt]	erwarten
to **experience** [ɪkˈspɪəriəns]	erleben
explanation [ˌekspləˈneɪʃn]	Erklärung
extension [ɪkˈstenʃn]	Anschluss, Apparat
extensive [ɪkˈstensɪv]	umfassend, umfangreich

F

face to face [ˌfeɪs tə ˈfeɪs]	im persönlichen Kontakt
familiar, to sound ~	vertraut klingen,
[saʊnd fəˈmɪliə]	bekannt vorkommen
fault [fɔːlt]	Fehler, Schuld
feature [ˈfiːtʃə]	Merkmal, Eigenschaft
fee [fiː]	Gebühr, Honorar
feedback [ˈfiːdbæk]	Rückmeldung
feeling [ˈfiːlɪŋ]	Gefühl
file [faɪl]	Datei
to **fill in** [ˌfɪl ˈɪn]	ausfüllen
to **flag** [flæg]	kennzeichnen, markieren
flow chart [ˈfləʊ tʃɑːt]	Flussdiagramm
fluent [ˈfluːənt]	fließend
to **focus on** [ˈfəʊkəs ɒn]	sich konzentrieren auf

to **follow** [ˈfɒləʊ]	folgen
follow-through [ˌfɒləʊ ˈθruː]	Durchführung
follow-up [ˈfɒləʊ ʌp]	Nachbetreuung
form letter [ˈfɔːm letə]	Serienbrief
free of charge [friː əv tʃɑːdʒ]	kostenlos
to **freeze** [friːz]	erstarren, stehen bleiben
frequent [ˈfriːkwənt]	häufig, Viel-
to **frown** [fraʊn]	(die Stirn) runzeln
frustration [frʌˈstreɪʃn]	Enttäuschung

G

to **generate** [ˈdʒenəreɪt]	erzeugen, erzielen
to **get back to** [get ˈbæk tə]	zurückrufen, sich wieder melden
to **get through** [ˌget ˈθruː]	durchkommen (am Telefon)
to **go over** [ˌgəʊ ˈəʊvə]	durchgehen
to **go on over** [ˌgəʊ ɒn ˈəʊvə]	hinübergehen
grateful [ˈgreɪtfl]	dankbar
grooming [ˈgruːmɪŋ]	Körperpflege
guarantee [ˌgærənˈtiː]	Garantie

H

hand-held computer	PDA
[ˌhændheld kəmˈpjuːtə]	
to **handle** [ˈhændl]	erledigen, bearbeiten
to **hang up** [ˌhæŋ ˈʌp]	auflegen
helpline [ˈhelplaɪn]	Telefonberatung, Notrufstelle
to **hesitate** [ˈhezɪteɪt]	zögern
highlight [ˈhaɪlaɪt]	Höhepunkt
high-tech [ˌhaɪ ˈtek]	Hightech-, hoch technisiert
to **hold** [həʊld]	warten, am Apparat bleiben
hold, to put on ~ [pʊt ɒn ˈhəʊld]	(am Telefon) warten lassen
hospitality [ˌhɒspɪˈtæləti]	Gastfreundschaft, Bewirtung
house, open ~ [ˌəʊpən ˈhaʊs]	offenes Haus
hurry, to be in a ~ [bi ɪn ə ˈhʌri]	es eilig haben

I

ice, to break the ~ [ˌbreɪk ði ˈaɪs]	das Eis brechen
to **ignore** [ɪgˈnɔː]	ignorieren, nicht beachten
immediately [ɪˈmiːdiətli]	sofort, umgehend
impact [ˈɪmpækt]	(Aus-)Wirkung, Effekt
impatient [ɪmˈpeɪʃnt]	ungeduldig
impression [ɪmˈpreʃn]	Eindruck
impressive [ɪmˈpresɪv]	beeindruckend, eindrucksvoll
incentive [ɪnˈsentɪv]	Anreiz
incident [ˈɪnsɪdənt]	Vorgang, Zwischenfall
inconvenienced, to be ~ by	Umstände bereiten
[bi ˌɪnkənˈviːniənst baɪ]	
to **inhale** [ɪnˈheɪl]	inhalieren, einatmen
insecure [ˌɪnsɪˈkjʊə]	unsicher
to **install** [ɪnˈstɔːl]	installieren, anschließen
instant [ˈɪnstənt]	sofortig, umgehend
instantly [ˈɪnstəntli]	sofort
instead [ɪnˈsted]	stattdessen
insulting [ɪnˈsʌltɪŋ]	beleidigend
intention [ɪnˈtenʃn]	Absicht
to **interrupt** [ˌɪntəˈrʌpt]	unterbrechen
interruption [ˌɪntəˈrʌpʃn]	Unterbrechung, Störung
introduce, to ~ oneself	sich (selbst) vorstellen
[ˌɪntrəˈdjuːs wʌnself]	
invisible [ɪnˈvɪzəbl]	unsichtbar
invitation [ˌɪnvɪˈteɪʃn]	Einladung
invoice [ˈɪnvɔɪs]	Rechnung
item [ˈaɪtəm]	Artikel, Gegenstand

J

jargon [ˈdʒɑːgən]	Fachsprache
jumper [ˈdʒʌmpə]	Pullover

L

latest [ˈleɪtɪst]	neueste/r/s
latter [ˈlætə]	letzte/r/s
to **launch** [lɔːntʃ]	herausbringen, einführen
leaflet [ˈliːflət]	Broschüre, Prospekt
to **lease** [liːs]	mieten

least, the ~ [ðə 'liːst] — das Mindeste
location [ləʊ'keɪʃn] — (Stand-)Ort, Lage
long, so ~ for now [səʊ 'lɒŋ fə naʊ] — bis bald
long-term [ˌlɒŋ 'tɜːm] — langfristig, Langzeit-
to **look up** [ˌlʊk 'ʌp] — heraussuchen

M

mail, junk ~ ['dʒʌŋk meɪl] — Werbemüll
mailing list ['meɪlɪŋ lɪst] — Adressenliste
to **make sure** [ˌmeɪk 'ʃʊə] — sicherstellen
manual ['mænjuəl] — Handbuch
manufacturing [ˌmænju'fæktʃərɪŋ] — Produktion
to **matter** ['mætə] — von Bedeutung sein, darauf ankommen
meantime, in the ~ [ɪn ðə 'miːntaɪm] — in der Zwischenzeit
to **memorize** ['meməraɪz] — auswendig lernen
to **mention** ['menʃn] — erwähnen, nennen
mind, to change my ~ [ˌtʃeɪndʒ maɪ 'maɪnd] — meine Meinung ändern, es mir anders überlegen
misleading [ˌmɪs'liːdɪŋ] — irreführend
misunderstanding [ˌmɪsʌndə'stændɪŋ] — Missverständnis
mix-up ['mɪks ʌp] — Missverständnis, Verwechslung
moreover [mɔːr'əʊvə] — zudem
mouse, to be a ~ click away [bi ə 'maʊs klɪk əweɪ] — (nur) einen Mausklick entfernt sein
to **network** ['netwɜːk] — zusammenarbeiten, sich abstimmen

N

news flash ['njuːz flæʃ] — Kurzmeldung(en)
nowadays ['naʊədeɪz] — heutzutage

O

to **offer** ['ɒfə] — (an)bieten
once [wʌns] — einmal
operating system ['ɒpəreɪtɪŋ sɪstəm] — Betriebssystem
operator ['ɒpəreɪtə] — Telefonist/in, (Telefon-)Vermittlung
opinion [ə'pɪnɪən] — Meinung, Ansicht
order entry clerk [ˌɔːdər 'entri klɑːk] — Angestellte/r für die Auftragserfassung
order, to place an ~ [ˌpleɪs ən 'ɔːdə] — einen Auftrag erteilen, eine Bestellung aufgeben
otherwise ['ʌðəwaɪz] — sonst, ansonsten
outcome ['aʊtkʌm] — Resultat, Ergebnis
outlook ['aʊtlʊk] — Vorhersage, Ausblick
to **overcharge** [ˌəʊvə'tʃɑːdʒ] — zuviel berechnen
overlooked, to get ~ [get ˌəʊvə'lʊkt] — übersehen werden
oversight ['əʊvəsaɪt] — Versehen
overview ['əʊvəvjuː] — Überblick, -sicht
to **overwhelm** [ˌəʊvə'welm] — überfordern

P

package holiday ['pækɪdʒ hɒlədeɪ] — Pauschalreise
paragraph ['pærəgrɑːf] — Absatz
particular [pə'tɪkjələ] — bestimmt, speziell
partnership ['pɑːtnəʃɪp] — Kombination
password ['pɑːswɜːd] — Passwort
patient ['peɪʃnt] — geduldig
people skills ['piːpl skɪlz] — Fähigkeiten im Umgang mit Menschen
perception [pə'sepʃn] — Wahrnehmung
to **perform** [pə'fɔːm] — durchführen, arbeiten
pleasant ['pleznt] — angenehm, freundlich
pleasure, my ~ [maɪ 'pleʒə] — gern geschehen
point [pɔɪnt] — Standpunkt
policy ['pɒləsi] — (Firmen-)Politik

polite [pə'laɪt] — höflich
position [pə'zɪʃn] — Stellung
possibility [ˌpɒsə'bɪləti] — Möglichkeit
postcode ['pəʊstkəʊd] — Postleitzahl
potential [pə'tenʃl] — möglich, potenziell
prepared, to be ~ [bi prɪ'peəd] — bereit sein
pressure, under ~ [ˌʌndə 'preʃə] — unter Druck
to **pretend** [prɪ'tend] — vorgeben, so tun als ob
preview ['priːvjuː] — Vorschau
priority [praɪ'ɒrəti] — Vorrang, Priorität
to **process** ['prəʊses] — bearbeiten
productive [prə'dʌktɪv] — produktiv
profit ['prɒfɪt] — Profit, Gewinn
promise ['prɒmɪs] — Versprechen
promotional [prə'məʊʃənl] — Werbe-
prompt [prɒmpt] — sofort, unverzüglich
prompt, to be ~ in [bi 'prɒmpt ɪn] — (etw) umgehend tun
promptly ['prɒmptli] — zügig
proud, to be ~ of [bi 'praʊd əv] — stolz sein auf
to **provide** [prə'vaɪd] — (an)bieten
to **pull up** [ˌpʊl 'ʌp] — aufrufen
punctuation [ˌpʌŋktʃu'eɪʃn] — Zeichensetzung, Interpunktion
to **put through** [ˌpʊt 'θruː] — verbinden, durchstellen

Q

questionnaire [ˌkwestʃə'neə] — Fragebogen
quote [kwəʊt] — Angebot, Kostenvoranschlag; Zitat

R

range [reɪndʒ] — (Waren-)Sortiment, Palette
rapport [ræ'pɔː] — (enges) Verhältnis
rate [reɪt] — Tarif
to **rate** [reɪt] — bewerten, einstufen
to **reach** [riːtʃ] — erreichen
to **react** [ri'ækt] — reagieren
to **realize** ['rɪəlaɪz] — (be)merken, sich bewusst werden/sein
receipt [rɪ'siːt] — Quittung, Beleg
receiver [rɪ'siːvə] — (Telefon-)Hörer
to **recommend** [ˌrekə'mend] — empfehlen
to **refer (to)** [rɪ'fɜː tə] — verweisen (auf)
reference ['refərəns] — Bezug
refund ['riːfʌnd] — Rückerstattung
to **refund** [rɪ'fʌnd] — (zurück)erstatten
regard, in ~ to [ɪn rɪ'gɑːd tə] — in Bezug auf
regional ['riːdʒənl] — regional
to **register** ['redʒɪstə] — registrieren, eintragen (lassen)
register ['redʒɪstə] — Stilebene
to **regret** [rɪ'gret] — bedauern
regular ['regjələ] — regelmäßig, Stamm-
relocation [ˌriːləʊ'keɪʃn] — Umzug
to **renew** [rɪ'njuː] — erneuern
to **replace** [rɪ'pleɪs] — ersetzen
replacement [rɪ'pleɪsmənt] — Ersatz
report [rɪ'pɔːt] — Bericht
request [rɪ'kwest] — Bitte, Wunsch, Anfrage
required, to be ~ [bi rɪ'kwaɪəd] — erforderlich sein
to **resolve** [rɪ'zɒlv] — klären, lösen
resort [rɪ'zɔːt] — Ferienort, Urlaubsort
responsible, to be ~ for [rɪ'spɒnsəbl] — verantwortlich sein für
responsibility, to take ~ [teɪk rɪˌspɒnsə'bɪləti] — Verantwortung übernehmen
rest, to get ~ [get 'rest] — Ruhe finden
retail ['riːteɪl] — Einzelhandel
revenue ['revənjuː] — Einkünfte, Einnahmen
to **review** [rɪ'vjuː] — einen Überblick geben, überprüfen
rude [ruːd] — unhöflich
to **ruin** ['ruːɪn] — ruinieren

runaround, to give sb the ~ [gɪv ðə 'rʌnəraʊnd] — jdn an der Nase herumführen, hinhalten

to rush [rʌʃ] — sich beeilen (mit)

rush order [rʌʃ 'ɔːdə] — Eilauftrag

S

salutation [ˌsælju'teɪʃn] — Anrede

satisfaction [ˌsætɪs'fækʃn] — Zufriedenheit

schedule ['ʃedjuːl] — Zeitplan

scrambled ['skræmbld] — verstümmelt, durcheinander

screen [skriːn] — Bildschirm

script [skrɪpt] — Text, Manuskript

security precaution [sɪˌkjʊərəti prɪ'kɔːʃn] — Vorsichtsmaßnahme, Sicherheitsvorkehrung

selection [sɪ'lekʃn] — Auswahl

service ['sɜːvɪs] — Dienst(leistung)

to service ['sɜːvɪs] — reinigen, putzen, versorgen

service, to give good/bad ~ [gɪv ˌgʊd, ˌbæd 'sɜːvɪs] — guten/schlechten Kundendienst leisten

service line ['sɜːvɪs laɪn] — Dienstleistungsangebot

to set up [ˌset 'ʌp] — vereinbaren

setting, text ~ ['tekst setɪŋ] — Textsatz

sharply ['ʃɑːpli] — gereizt

shipment ['ʃɪpmənt] — Lieferung

to sign up [ˌsaɪn 'ʌp] — (sich) einschreiben

signal, engaged ~ [ɪnˌgeɪdʒd 'sɪgnəl] — Besetztzeichen

to sip [sɪp] — schlürfen

to slam down [ˌslæm 'daʊn] — hinknallen

small talk ['smɔːl tɔːk] — höfliche Konversation

to soften ['sɒfn] — abschwächen

solution [sə'luːʃn] — Lösung

spare part [ˌspeə 'pɑːt] — Ersatzteil

to speak up [ˌspiːk 'ʌp] — laut(er) sprechen

specific [spə'sɪfɪk] — genau, präzise

specification [ˌspesɪfɪ'keɪʃn] — Angabe, (technische Spezifikation)

speedy ['spiːdi] — schnell, rasch

spellchecker ['speltʃekə] — Rechtschreibprogramm

to stand for ['stænd fə] — stehen für

standard ['stændəd] — normal, üblich

startling ['stɑːtlɪŋ] — erschreckend

statement ['steɪtmənt] — Aussage

stock, to be in ~ [bi ɪn 'stɒk] — vorrätig sein

to stop by [ˌstɒp 'baɪ] — vorbeikommen, -schauen

straight away [streɪt ə'weɪ] — umgehend

strong [strɒŋ] — stark

subscriber [səb'skraɪbə] — Kunde/Kundin, Abonnent/in

success story [sək'ses stɔːri] — Erfolgsgeschichte

successful [sək'sesfl] — erfolgreich

to suggest [sə'dʒest] — vorschlagen

suggestion [sə'dʒestʃən] — Vorschlag

to suit [suːt] — passen

suitable ['suːtəbl] — geeignet, passend

to sum up [ˌsʌm 'ʌp] — zusammenfassen

supervisor ['suːpəvaɪzə] — Vorgesetzte/r

survey ['sɜːveɪ] — (Meinungs-)Umfrage, Untersuchung

system requirement [sɪstəm rɪ'kwaɪəmənt] — Systemanforderung

T

tact [tækt] — Takt

to take the time [teɪk ðə 'taɪm] — sich Zeit nehmen

team [tiːm] — Mannschaft

technician [tek'nɪʃn] — Techniker/in

telephone manner ['telɪfəʊn mænə] — Verhalten/Umgangsformen am Telefon

teller ['telə] — (Bank)Kassierer/in

tip [tɪp] — Hinweis, Tipp

tool [tuːl] — Instrument/Werkzeug

totally ['təʊtəli] — völlig

touch, to get in ~ [get ɪn 'tʌtʃ] — (sich) in Verbindung setzen

tournament ['tʊənəmənt] — Turnier

to track [træk] — suchen, auffinden, verfolgen

trade fair ['treɪd feə] — Handelsmesse

transaction [træn'zækʃn] — Geschäft(sabschluss), Transaktion

transfer ['trænsfɜː] — Überweisung

to transfer [træns'fɜː] — durchstellen, weitervermitteln

trend [trend] — Trend, Tendenz

troubled, to look ~ [lʊk 'trʌbld] — besorgt aussehen

troubleshooting ['trʌblʃuːtɪŋ] — Fehlersuche, -behebung

turn-around time ['tɜːn əraʊnd] — Bearbeitungszeit

U

unacceptable [ˌʌnək'septəbl] — unannehmbar, inakzeptabel

uncomfortable [ʌn'kʌmftəbl] — unbequem

unique selling point (USP) [juːˌniːk 'selɪŋ pɔɪnt] — USP, Alleinstellungsmerkmal

unsatisfactory [ˌʌnˌsætɪs'fæktəri] — unbefriedigend

up and running [ʌp ən 'rʌnɪŋ] — funktionstüchtig, in Gang

to update [ʌp'deɪt] — aktualisieren, erneuern

to upgrade [ˌʌp'greɪd] — aufrüsten

urgent ['ɜːdʒənt] — dringend, eilig

used, to get ~ to [get 'juːstə] — sich gewöhnen an

useless ['juːsləs] — nutzlos, sinnlos

V

valued ['væljuːd] — geschätzt

view, point of ~ [ˌpɔɪnt əv 'vjuː] — Standpunkt, Ansicht

voicemail ['vɔɪsmeɪl] — Mailbox

voucher ['vaʊtʃə] — Gutschein

W

to waste [weɪst] — vergeuden, verschwenden

well-known [ˌwel 'nəʊn] — sehr bekannt, berühmt

wronged [rɒŋd] — ungerecht behandelt

Y

to yell at sb ['jel ət] — jdn anschreien

Useful phrases and vocabulary

Basic socializing

Greetings and introductions
Good morning. You must be ...
It's nice to finally meet you face to face.
→ It's good/nice to meet you, too.
I'd like you to meet ...
Anke, this is ...
I'd like to introduce you to ...
May I introduce myself? I'm ...
→ Nice to meet you. I'm ...

Small talk questions
How was your trip (AE)/journey (BE)/flight?
Did you find us OK?
Did you have any trouble finding us?
And is this your first time in Hamburg?
So, have you ever been to Hamburg before?
So, how's your hotel? Everything OK?
Great weather, isn't it?
How was the weather in London?
Oh, are you interested in tennis?

Offering hospitality
May I take your coat?
Let me help you with that.
→ Oh, that's very kind of you.
So, if you would like to take a seat ...
Please take a seat.
→ Thank you.
Would you care for coffee or tea?
Would you like some coffee or tea?
→ Yes, please. Tea would be nice.
Can I get you some mineral water?
No, thank you.
Can I get you something else? Juice, perhaps?

Saying goodbye
Thanks for stopping by.
Thanks for a good meeting.
It was great to meet (both of) you.
Have a good trip (AE)/journey (BE).
So long for now.
Goodbye./Bye.

General conversation

Asking for clarification
I'm sorry, but I didn't (quite) catch that/understand you exactly.
Could we go over that once more?
Could you repeat that, please?
Could you speak a bit slower/more slowly, please?

Making suggestions
Why don't you/we ... ?
Don't/Wouldn't you agree that ... ?
Isn't it a better idea to ... ?
It makes a good/bad impression if you ...

Responding to suggestions
That's right. / I agree.
I see your point.
I disagree because ...
I don't agree. I would ...

Customer meetings

Thanks for coming today.
As I understand it, you'd like to discuss ...
I've done some research into your company. It seems you ... . Is that right?
So, that was my suggestion. Is that suitable for you? I'd like to get your feedback.
Let's go over the action points once more. I want to be sure we agree.
I'll see what we can do.

Trade fairs

Starting a conversation
Excuse me, may I help you?
→ No, thanks. I'm just looking/browsing.
How can I help you?
May I introduce myself? I'm ...
→ Nice/Pleased to meet you. I'm ...
Could I ask your name?
→ My name's ...
How are you enjoying the fair?
→ It's very interesting. It's a good chance to network.

Talking business

Are you looking for anything special/in particular?
→ I'm looking for/interested in …
Could I offer you/interest you in … ?
→ Yes, I'd like to have your latest brochure/
catalogue/price list.
Please feel free to ask me any questions.
Would you mind if I … phoned/emailed/contacted
you?
May I give you my card?
→ Of course. And here's mine. I look forward to
hearing from you …

Ending the conversation

It was so nice to meet you.
I hope you enjoy the fair.
→ Thanks, it was a pleasure. I appreciate your help.

Presentations

Welcoming/Introducing

I'd like to welcome you to …
Thank you for coming today.
My name's …
I work for … and I'm in charge of/responsible for …

Introducing the subject

I'd like to give you a short preview of my
presentation …
We'd like to introduce/show you/help you get to
know our latest …

Describing products and services

Our product/service range includes …
The special highlights are …

Explaining the unique selling points (USPs)

We stand out from our competitors because …
Our USPs are …

Giving promotional information

Please feel free to pick up/take a brochure/leaflet/
free sample.
We've got our promotional information and samples
available here.

Offering incentives to try a product

I'd like to offer a special introductory price.
We can offer you a discount if you order today.

Offering follow-up

I'll be glad/pleased to send you … by next Monday.
I'll be in contact/touch with you in two weeks.
I/We look forward to doing business with you.

Inviting/appreciating new customers

We'd be pleased/glad to have you as a new
customer.
We'd welcome the chance to do business with your
company.

Summarizing

I'd just like to sum up the main points of today's
presentation.
Thank you for your kind attention.

Telephoning

Identifying yourself (person called)

Good morning. Apex industries.
Hello, Martha Greer speaking. How can/may I help
you?

Identifying yourself (caller)

Hello, my name is … . I'm with ABC AG in Bonn.
This is Joan Everts from Everts, Samuels and Barker.
Hello, I'd like to introduce myself.
I'm calling to …

Getting through

I'd like to speak to John, please.
Could you put me through to John, please?
→ Of course, one moment please.
→ Thanks for holding/waiting. I'm putting you
through to John's office now.

Messages

Would you like to leave a message?
→ That's OK. I'll call back later.
Could I leave her a message to ring me back as
soon as possible?
→ I'll make sure she gets your message straight
away.
→ I'll make sure he calls you back today.

Showing attention

I'll just write that down.
Let me just make a note of that.
I've got your customer file right in front of me.
I'm checking your file as we speak.

Confirming information
Can I just go over/confirm the details again?
Let's go over it again to be sure of the details.

Explaining action
I'll be glad to send this out to you today.
You should receive it by …

Showing follow-up
I'll check on that information with my colleague and
 call you back in two hours.
I'll make sure that he/she calls you back today.

Finishing the call
Could I help/assist you with anything else today?
Can I take care of anything else for you?
Is there anything else I can help you with today?
I appreciate you taking the time to talk to me.
Many thanks for calling us.

Making arrangements

Asking for an appointment
Could we schedule an appointment?
Are you available/free on Monday?
Does next Thursday suit you?
How about 2 pm on Tuesday?

Agreeing on a time
Just let me check my diary/planner.
Yes, Tuesday is fine with me.
Sounds good. Tuesday at 2 pm then.

Suggesting a new time
I'm sorry, but I've got another engagement.
How about Tuesday morning instead?
Actually, Thursday morning would work out/be
 better for me.

Confirming
OK, we'll see each other next Thursday at 11.00 at
 your office.
Could you confirm the details in an email?
Here is my mobile number in case you need to
 reach me.
I look forward to seeing you (then).

Call centre phone calls

Offering assistance
How can I help you today?
What can I do for you?

Understanding customers
I see. So, as I understand it, … . Is that correct?
Let me just repeat that.

Confirming details
Could I just have your name and address, please?
I'd just like to confirm your contact details.
Could I go over your order again?

Making promises and keeping them
Your order will go out overnight today.
I'll call you back in half an hour.
I will personally make sure …

Agreeing on action
Does that sound all right?
Do you have any other questions?
I hope this is to your satisfaction.

Following up and following through
I'll ring you when the technician has finished the
 repair work to make sure everything is all right.

Troubleshooting
So, what exactly is the problem?
Could you explain the problem in more detail?
Could you explain what you've done so far?
Let me just talk you through the steps.
Do you follow that so far?
Do you have any questions so far?
Can you see that all right?
Is everything clear up to now?
→ What exactly does OS stand for?
→ What do you mean exactly?
→ Sorry, what does that mean?
That means you need to have …
In other words, you need to have …
This is what I'm going to do: …

Problems and complaints

Apologizing
First of all, I'm so/terribly sorry about that.
I apologize for …
Let me apologize …

Clarifying the information
Could you tell me exactly what happened?
Could you explain a bit more …?
Do you mind if I just go over that again …?

Listening carefully
I'll just make a few notes as you speak.
I'm just taking this down.

Showing empathy
I understand./I see what you mean.
I would feel the same way.
I can understand the reason for your complaint.
What a difficult situation this puts you in.

Taking responsibility
There seems to be a misunderstanding.
It appears that your order got overlooked.
I'm afraid there has been some sort of mix-up.
It looks like an oversight on our part.
It seems (that) the order was not handled promptly
   enough.
It appears (that) a mistake has been made.

Saying how and when the problem will be solved
I'll take care of this for you at once.
I'll get back to you straight away.
You'll receive (a refund/replacement) by tomorrow ...
I'm sure we can find a solution.
I'd be glad to offer you ... to make up for this
   inconvenience.
This should be resolved by the end of today.

Offering an alternative
If this solution does not meet your needs, then I
   can suggest ... as an alternative.
I'll look into other possibilities by ...

Summarizing the discussion
What we have decided is ...
Our action plan is ...
I'd like to go over this once more to make sure we
   agree.

Assuring the client of follow-up
I'll get back to you in/by ...
I'll follow up to make sure that ...

Ending with a friendly, helpful tone
I hope you are satisfied with the outcome.
Thank you for bringing this to our attention.
Is there anything else I can help you with today?
Don't hesitate to ring again if there are any more
   problems.

Dealing with complaints in writing (formal)
We very much regret ...
We are very concerned to hear that ...
We assure you that we are doing everything
   we can ...
The problem has now been resolved.
Once again, we apologize for the inconvenience.
We (do) value your business and hope to keep you
   as a long-term customer.

Letter and email writing (formal/less formal)

Connecting with the reader
In reference to your letter/email of ...
In/With regard to your phone call ...
Further to our recent meeting ...
Re your letter/email of ...
Thanks for your phone call this morning.
I hope everything is going well.

Reason for writing
We are writing to confirm ...
I am writing to let you know ...
I would like to inform you ...
I'm just writing to tell you ...
I'd like to let you know ...
Just a quick email to let you know ...

Enclosures
Please find enclosed the price list you requested.
In the enclosed information packet, you will find
   product descriptions, ...
As you will see from the enclosed brochure, ...

Attachments
I'm sending you the current price list as an
   attachment.
I've attached the specifications as a pdf document.
Please complete the attached form and return it to
   us.
Here is the file you asked for.

Giving good news
We are pleased to say ...
I am delighted to inform you ...
I'm happy to tell you ...
I'm glad to tell you ...

Requests

We would be grateful if we could ...
I would appreciate it if we could ...
It'd be great if we could ...
Could you ... ?

Taking action

I will phone you/contact you ...
We would be delighted/pleased to assist you.
I'll get in touch with you/get back to you ...
I'd be glad to help out.

Concluding

If you have any further questions, please do not
    hesitate to contact me.
If you have any other questions, please contact me.
We look forward to hearing from/meeting you soon.
I look forward to seeing you next week.
Let me know if you need anything else/any other
    help.
Look(ing) forward to your reply/to hearing from
    you.
Look(ing) forward to seeing you next week.

Useful Verbs (in context)

to apologize	We apologize for the mix-up with the invoice.	sich entschuldigen
to appreciate	We appreciate you as a valuable customer.	zu schätzen wissen
to assist	How can I assist you with your order today?	helfen
to assure	I can assure you that you will receive a refund by Friday.	zusichern
to be grateful	We would be grateful if you could contact us soon.	dankbar sein für
to be in charge of	Can you tell me who is in charge of this account?	verantwortlich sein
to be responsible for	I am responsible for (taking) all of your orders.	verantwortlich sein
to care for sth	Would you care for a drink?	möchten
to catch	I didn't catch that. Could you say it again?	verstehen
to confirm	Let me just confirm your contact details.	bestätigen
to deal with	I'll connect you with somebody who deals with that.	sich kümmern um
to follow through	We follow through on every customer request.	etw zu Ende führen
to follow up	I am writing to follow up on our phone call yesterday.	etw weiterfolgen
to get back to sb	I'll make sure she gets back to you by Friday.	sich bei jdm wieder melden
to get through to	I'm sorry you were unable to get through to the helpdesk.	durchkommen
to go over	I'll go over it again to make sure it's clear.	etw durchgehen
to hold	Could you hold or would you prefer to leave a message?	am Apparat bleiben
to inconvenience	We hope you have not been inconvenienced by the delay.	jdm Umstände machen
to inform	Please inform us as soon as you receive the package.	informieren
to look into sth	I'll look into your question and call you back in two hours.	etw prüfen
to put sb through	One moment, please. I'll put you through to the manager.	jdn durchstellen
to recommend	I'd like to recommend a solution for all your business needs.	empfehlen
to regret	I regret that this has caused you so many problems.	bedauern
to resolve	We will do everything possible to resolve the misunderstanding.	klären
to schedule	Could we schedule a time to meet next week?	vereinbaren
to stand out	We stand out from our competitors with our superior service.	sich abheben
to take care of sth	We try to take care of all complaints within 24 hours.	etw erledigen
to take sth down	One moment, I just need to take down your address.	etw aufschreiben
to talk sb through sth	I'll talk you through the steps to solve the problem.	etw durchsprechen